The LAUGH'S ON US

Cricket's Finest Tell Their Funniest

CARTOONS BY JEFF HOOK

SWAN
PUBLISHING

First published in 1989 by
Swan Publishing Pty Ltd
4 Childe St, Byron Bay, N.S.W. 2481

National Library of Australia
Cataloguing-in-Publication data.

The Laugh's On Us

ISBN 0 9587841 4 0

1. Cricket—humour. 2. Cricket—Anecdotes.
I. Hook, Jeff, 1928-

796.35'8'0207

Typeset by Midland Typesetters Pty Ltd
Printed in Australia by Griffin Press, Adelaide

Design: Stan Lamond, Lamond Art & Design

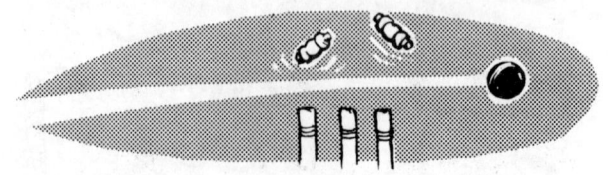

CONTENTS

by
Richie
Benaud

FOREWORD

HUMOUR is many things to many people in every walk of life, some see it as being ribald, some understated, there are those who delight in the belly laugh or the sense of the ridiculous, others much prefer the one-liner. There are situations which provide such obvious humour that everyone will laugh or smile and there are those which are humourous because they are embarrassing.

In the following pages there are many stories which cover the areas of humour mentioned above and they have all happened at some time. It may even be that you have found yourself in the same situation as one of the cricketers telling the story, not that this would be unusual because stories of cricketers and cricket stories are almost as old as humour itself. Back before the turn of the century we have tales of those who played the game hard or with humour, or with the occasional sip of brewed liquid to keep them going. They, and the disasters or fun that came their way, are all part of the game.

The language of sportsmen differs in intensity from country to country, from level to level, so too does the vehemence of the reply. In the pressure of the final day of the Old Trafford Test of 1956, Jim Laker was on his way to taking 19 wickets in the game. At the other end Tony Lock had taken only one and the frustration of that, and some prudent, time-wasting work I was doing tapping down dents in the pitch, saw him, momentarily snap.

As he gathered in another forward prod he let fly with a return to Godfrey Evans which whipped past my ear and thudded into the glove. "Tap that one down you bastard," floated down the pitch. At tea time The Rev. David Shepherd whipped just as quickly into our dressing-room to apologise for the profanity on the field. Ah! They were the days, but, sitting sipping a cup of tea, I'd actually forgotten the incident so hard were we all concentrating, and I didn't blame 'Lockie' one little bit!

It was said once of golf that if profanity had any influence on the flight of the ball the game would be played far better than it is. So it is with many sports. From Presidents to chimney sweeps they come and go and there is a story in everyone who steps on to a sporting field. Some sportsmen are even dangerous. President Gerald Ford, a notorious snap-hooker and wild slicer off the tee, was heard to proclaim one day that he knew his golf was improving every time he stopped hitting spectators.

That kind of thing would always be embarrassing for a President, but so long as he was able to laugh about his problem, and so long as no lasting damage was done to the hapless spectators, no harm was done.

Embarrassment of another kind came my way one night in London where Daphne and I had attended a splendid dinner hosted by the late David Kenning, an outstanding BBC television sports producer.

At the dinner were 'Slim' Wilkinson and his wife.

'Slim' was then Head of BBC Sport and a Very, VIP. They drove us home and when we arrived there, your correspondent, awakened from a doze and forgetting we were not in a taxi, thrust his hand into a pocket, pulled out a fiver and shoved it at the Head of Sport with the time-honoured words, "Thanks pal, keep the rest to buy a drink."

Fortunately 'Slim' has a good sense of humour and I hope yours too will be attuned to the stories you read through these pages. Those who have written them work on the basis that life is too short to take oneself over seriously. It's a good maxim!

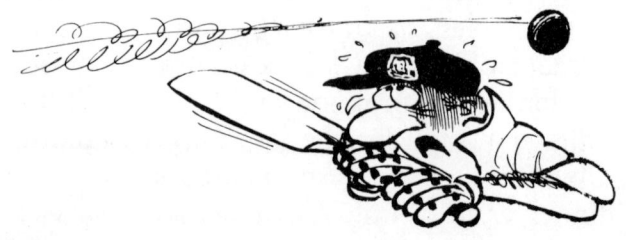

by
Allan
Border

GOING APE

I WAS not a part of Australia's tour of Zimbabwe in 1984, but the guys who were couldn't wait to tell me after they got back about Greg Ritchie and his chimpanzees. 'Fat Cat' as Greg is rather appropriately known, had become ill during the trip and required surgery. He was laid up in hospital until a couple of days before the team returned to Australia.

The last fixture was a limited-over match on the day of departure and Greg was well enough by this stage to go along to the ground and watch. He was approached by a lot of well-wishers inquiring about his health and one of them just happened to be a fellow who owned two chimps. He had quite a chat with Greg and invited him home during the lunch adjournment to see his prized pets.

It was love at first sight as far as 'Fat Cat' was concerned. He was fascinated by these shambling simians, so much so that he begged their owner to bring them back to the ground to meet his team-mates. The owner agreed on condition that it be after the game when the crowd had dispersed. They became over-excited if there were a lot of people around, he said.

At six o clock, Greg, his mate and two 200 pound chimpanzees left for the ground. 'Fat Cat' was agog

11

with anticipation. Boy was he going to frighten the hell out of his mates!

Having arrived, 'Fat Cat' snuck his guests in the back way to the Australian dressing-room. He led them through a small tunnel entrance, threw open the door—and let both leads go.

All hell broke loose. "Shit, gorillas!" someone shouted. In a spontaneous reaction, the players panicked and the chimps went wild. Grown men turned to jelly in a split second. The chimps careered around the room trying to grab the players, many of whom were naked. Their nudity didn't stop them jumping out of windows. David Boon, who was involved in the pandemonium, swears he saw guys run up walls.

By the time the owner had rounded up his chimps, the dressing-room had been reduced to a shambles. When order was eventually restored, and when suggestions of tar-and-feathering the perpetrator had been discussed and dismissed, a still-shaken team-mate said to Greg: "Jesus, you bastard, what did you do that for?"

Greg, who had enjoyed the performance enormously, grinned broadly. "To teach you that nobody monkeys around with the 'Fat Cat'," he said.

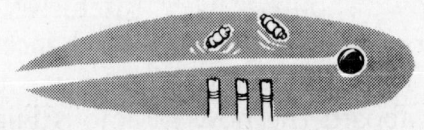

FAT CAT AND FRIENDS

'FAT CAT' as shown by my previous story, is a natural inclusion in any book dealing with the lighter side of cricket. I've no doubt the adventures and misadventures of Greg Ritchie alone would comfortably fill a good-sized book.

He has long been the comic of the Queensland team. He is a very funny man who can find humour in most situations.

'Fat Cat' likes a beer and leaves very little on his dinner plate. Hence his girth, a feature which does not go unnoticed by the quick-witted cricket fan.

We were in the field in a Sheffield Shield match in Adelaide in the 1988–89 season and play was interrupted by an injury to David Hookes. Greg took the opportunity to relax at his customary position at first slip and take in the scenery. His attention was captured by a flock of seagulls and his eyes followed their flight overhead. "Hey, Ritchie," yelled a sharp fan from the outer, "you can't eat the seagulls here!"

The laughter was unanimous.

We ribbed Greg about the comment for the next week while we were on tour. Our next match was at Newcastle and as we were about to take the field against New South Wales, 'Fat Cat' asked for silence. We stopped, wondering what the hell he had in mind.

"Skip," he said solemnly, "I'd appreciate it very much if you'd send the 12th man out ahead of us to clear the ground of seagulls!"

We hadn't been out there half an hour when some wag in the crowd shouted: "Hey, Ritchie! What about standing side-on and giving the grass a chance to grow!"

One thing 'Fat Cat' found amusing was the sequel to the drama aboard the now infamous Flight 55 to

Perth in 1988. Greg and Ian Botham went to court over the incident. As a result of the events, Ian was sacked by the Queensland Cricket Association. Greg was cleared—but it took him a whole season, until after our last Shield match in 1989, to crack a joke about the episode.

The game was in Perth and he was wary about the reception that might be awaiting him; so wary that he spent his non-cricket time in his hotel room. Greg has a fear of flying, but he was first on the plane for the flight back to Brisbane after the match. More than a little edgy, was 'Fat Cat'.

The looks the West Australian passengers boarding the plane gave him made it clear that Flight 55 was still very fresh in their minds, but Greg had obviously made plans of his own because he sat down and put his Queensland helmet on! The W.A. people looked down their noses at him and we got a fit of the giggles.

'Fat Cat' didn't crack a smile at any stage, but he timed his "run" to perfection. As we taxied out on to the runway, he stood, faced his fellow passengers and said, right out loud: "ISN'T IAN BOTHAM ON THIS PLANE???"

by
Frank
Tyson

A Foony Game Indeed

IF we accept the dictum, ad nauseam, that cricket is a 'foony game', and if we swallow unquestioningly the explanation of the Shorter Oxford Dictionary that humour is "the faculty of perceiving and enjoying what is ludicrous and amusing", then the anecdotes about flannelled fools and their game should be real showstoppers. For they are comicality set in the context of a funny game.

But beware the dictionary which comes bearing glib explanatory gifts! The old stand-by reference book snobbishly embellishes its facile explanation with the footnote that all humour—and thus, by inference, cricket humour—"is less intellectual and more sympathetic than wit."

What the hell! I can live with that. I have travelled the professional cricket circuits and quaffed pints in innumerable club bars all around the world for almost a lifetime without unearthing more than half a dozen practising cricketers capable of spelling—let alone understanding the words "Attic-salt".

There have been, of course, exceptions to the general rule: flashes of spiritual lightning which occasionally illumine the common foothills of cricket humour with what the Reverend W. A. Spooner would have called

16

'shafts of wit'.

How about the time in 1979 when Mike Brearley's touring Pommie side was dismissed for a very cheap score by Western Australia on a Perth green-top? Seeking to console his men, the English skipper breezed into the dressing-room after the tourists' defeat with this intended verbal salve: "Don't worry lads! On that wicket even Don Bradman wouldn't have got runs!" Fast bowler Bob Willis looked up gloomily and loosed his rejoinder: "I should bloody well think he wouldn't. He was born in 1908. He must be 71 by now!"

One waits a lifetime however, for the opportunity which the doyen of English commentators, John Arlott, once exploited to the full when South Africa visited England in 1947. The tourists played Middlesex at Lord's, where their slow left-handed spin bowler, 'Tuffy' Mann twice dismissed the home county's skipper, George Mann, for scores only minimally above the minimum.

On the occasion of the second dismissal, Arlott went straight to the bard, Robbie Burns, declaiming as only he could, in his distinctive Basingstoke burr: "Oh of Mann's inhumanity to Mann."

Cricket humour, however, usually has nothing to do with such verbal gymnastics. It is more concerned with the John Cleesian brand of humour: fun which has its roots in the earthy characters of the game. The cricket joke generally pumps up eccentric players and odd situations to a homeric grandeur; and then, just as they reach climax of self-aggrandisement, it deflates them with a pin-prick.

Their pride is punctured to the accompaniment of the metaphoric raspberry of a whoopee cushion. If the comical anticlimax is at the expense of the narrator of the joke, the greater is the listener's enjoyment. At least so I've found—and I shall illustrate it with a Tyson story.

I go back to the 1950s and the days when my side, Northamptonshire, usually played Derbyshire away on the Racecourse ground in the county town. I can say unequivocally that while racehorses might have found the Derby hospitable, I certainly did not.

More often than not our games were conducted in a freezing wind which swept across the black heath. It was said that there was no high ground between the Russian Ural Mountains and the Derby ground to divert the icy blast—and I certainly believed that useless piece of geographical trivia.

The local curator, who inhabited a pavilion which seemed to be a cross between the Taj Mahal and a urinal on the Brighton promenade, had a quaint custom of preparing two pitches for the Northamptonshire game. One was brown and barren of grass and pace, in case I—then, by reputation, the fastest bowler in England—played.

The other was grassy green and lively, to help the more-than-useful home pace attack of Gladwin and Jackson, if I did not appear and Northants were reduced to an initial stock assault of medium pace.

The greatest enjoyment one obtained from a game at Derby was getting off the field to luxuriate in the hot water of one of the enormous antique bathtubs, which were the only comfortable legacy of the 19th century to the county's cricketers. After one typically frigid and unsuccessful day chasing the leather, I was soaking the old bones when the practical joker of the Northants team, roly-poly Yorkshireman, Des Barrick, entered the bathroom and without a word of warning poured a bucket of ice-cold water over my head!

Like most fast-bowlers, my strongest asset was my power of self-control and I restrained my immediate reaction to thump Barrick between the eyes. I waited until I was reheated, when I rose from my bath, dried myself and, armed with a retaliatory bucket of icy water, marched into the adjoining dressing room. There I proceeded to pour the contents of the bucket over Des's head—quite a sneaky trick, since he was now fully clothed!

Much to my amazement, Des burst out laughing! "I've got news for thee, Frank," he said. "I've just put your clothes on!" It was a very damp drive back to the team's hotel for me that night!

19

The personalities who enrich the English county cricket scene are a veritable Pandora's Box of humour. Umpire David Lloyd recounts the tale of an encounter with the ebullient Ian Botham while he was standing on a NatWest limited-over game between Somerset and Middlesex at Taunton.

When the last over of the match was about to be bowled, Somerset needed 24 runs for victory and Botham faced the daunting task of scoring them off Middlesex's ferocious West Indian paceman, Wayne Daniel.

The "Black Diamond", as Daniel was nicknamed, aimed his first delivery, a yorker, at leg-stump. Botham not only dug out the ball, he sent it soaring over the scoreboard at long-on for six!

As he raised his arms to signal the runs, Lloyd was still sceptical about Botham's ability to win the game. Eighteen runs were still needed off five balls! Botham then proceeded to shake Lloyd's scepticism and capture the complete attention of the many thousands of viewers watching the game on BBC Television. He despatched the next two deliveries for further sixes, over long-off and deep extra-cover!

Now Worcester required only six runs off the remaining three balls, and in the opinion of umpire Lloyd, "the game had reached a very interesting stage".

Imagine the surprise of the watchers when Botham, with ponderous deliberation, blocked the next two balls, one a full-toss and the other a half-volley.

Daniel's last ball was a beauty, a fast, good-length ball just outside off stump. The merit of the delivery did not even enter into Botham's reckoning. He simply stepped forward from his crease and swatted it contemptuously over the head of extra cover for the six runs needed for victory!

It was a beautifully stage-managed finish! And as Botham was striding off the ground he draped a massive muscular arm around the shoulders of David Lloyd. He pointed with his bat at the BBC television cameras stationed at long-on, "Stay with me, lad", he chortled, "and I'll make you famous on telly!"

The alleged feats of former England skipper, Mike Gatting, both on and off the field, are a rich source of apochryphal jokes in England in 1988. A fellow teacher told me the story of one of his history classes in a secondary school in Birmingham, a numerically large form which contained boys and girls of many races, Indians, West Indians, Pakistanis and Africans.

One day my colleague gave his pupils a history quiz. He explained that he would give them a quote made by a famous personality of the past and they had to tell him who made the remark, where and when.

His first quote was: "They now ring their bells, but they will soon wring their hands." Mohammad, a slightly-built Pakistani in the front row of the class shot up his hand. "Yes, Mohammad?" the teacher asked. "That Sir, was the expression credited to Sir Robert Walpole, the Prime Minister of England, on the out-break of war with Spain in 1739."

"That's excellent, Mohammad" the teacher said. The next quote was "We shall fight on the beaches; we shall fight on the landing grounds; we shall fight in the fields and in the streets; we shall fight in the hills; we shall never surrender." Once more the diminutive Pakistani was the first with his answer of Sir Winston Churchill, the Prime Minister of England, in a speech to the House of Commons in June, 1940.

As the teacher turned his back on the class to write

the answer on the blackboard, an anonymous voice from the back of the room exclaimed quite audibly: "Smart-arsed little Pakistani bastard!" Racism, thought the teacher as he whipped around to confront and demand of his class: "Who said that?"

Much to the teacher's amazement Mohammad's hand was instantly raised once more. "Yes, Mohammad?" he said testily.

"That Sir", said the little Paki, "Was Mike Gatting, the England cricket captain, to umpire Shanook Rana, Lahore, 1987!"

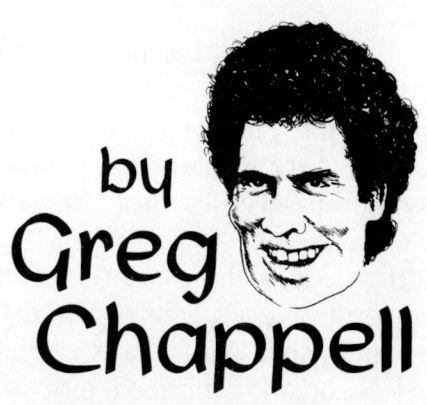

by Greg Chappell

JUST FOR THE RECORD

CRICKET ability (and he had plenty of that) aside, Ashley Mallett would have been worth his place in any Australian touring team of his era for entertainment value alone. I've met a lot of funny people in the best part of a lifetime in cricket, but 'Rowdy' stands alone as a man who could consistently reduce you to helpless mirth without even trying. His acts of mindless hilarity were very good for team morale.

Among other things, Ashley had a dread of flying, an unfortunate phobia for a jet-setting cricketer. He was the most nervous flier I have seen. Given a choice, he would always have travelled at night because that way he couldn't see how far he was above the ground.

Forced to fly by day, he would insist on a window seat so he could draw the shades and blot out the real world. If that meant begging a stranger to swap seats, then so be it. Strangers would usually agree but his team-mates, being more bloody-minded, would refuse to budge.

It sometimes reached the stage of 'Rowdy' appealing to the stewardess, even the captain, to have another player moved from his window seat.

I sat next to Ashley on a flight from Adelaide to Sydney in 1972, the first leg of the Ashes trip to

England. 'Rowdy', Jeff Hammond and I were the only members of the touring party on that flight, Ian Chappell having already left for England via the Caribbean.

Ashley hadn't slept well, was at the airport early and bought a copy of every metropolitan newspaper which had been published Australia-wide that morning. As we waited to board, I noticed him writing in a little book. He told me he was going to keep a diary of the tour and showed me the first entry: "6.00am. Arrived Adelaide Airport to catch F1. TN21 to Sydney".

Once aboard, Ashley quickly established himself in a window seat, drew the blind, arranged his newspapers in his lap, put a cigarette in his mouth in readiness for the no-smoking sign to be switched off and made his next diary entry: "6.45am. Boarded F1. TN21."

After take-off 'Rowdy' nervously busied himself in *The Sydney Morning Herald*, lit his cigarette and ordered a nerve-settling double scotch as he made his next entry: "7.10am F1. TN21 leaves Adelaide for Sydney."

To say Ashley Mallett is untidy is like accusing a pig of being dirty. Within 10 minutes he had news-papers spread all about him, clearly infringing into my neatly-defined space. Just as I dozed off, I was woken by a mad flurry to my left. It was 'Rowdy' putting out a fire he had started in his lap by dropping his second cigarette into his copy of the Adelaide *Advertiser*. And having beaten out the flames he made the next entry in his diary: "7.45am. Set fire to the Advertiser."

As the breakfast dishes were cleared I was almost tipped into the aisle by Ashley trying to jump to his feet as the hot tip of another cigarette fell into his lap. He was restrained by a very tightly-strapped seat belt and he had no fear of fire this time because he had simultaneously doused his lap by knocking over his second double scotch.

By this time I was immune to any disturbance on my immediate left, but I was curious when, several minutes later, he began through a mass of newspapers and other paraphernalia he had amassed in his lap, at his feet and all around him. I could see he was losing patience.

Eventually, he snatched up his pen and scribbled something on the top corner of his Melbourne *Age*: "8.15am. Lost Diary."

EXCUSE HIS BLEEPS

JEFFREY Robert Thomson was born to bowl fast. No-one in my experience was better equipped to be a fast bowler. He was strongly built, could run, jump and throw as well as the best and his flexibility was amazing. If he'd had the ambition, I think he could have been a great decathlete—and I daresay there are a lot of batsmen who wish he had been.

As well as sending down a lot of stinging deliveries, 'Thommo' handed out a few verbal bouncers in his time—and not all were aimed at opposition batsmen. Many were directed at himself, but one of his best was delivered to the hapless operator of the Sydney Cricket Ground electronic scoreboard.

Towards the end of the 1983–84 season—'Thommo' was bowling from the Randwick end at a vital stage of the game between Queensland and New South Wales. As he strove for extra pace he overstepped the mark and was no-balled. The next ball was the last of the over and the last before tea. As we left the ground, the electronic scoreboard exploded into life. "Congratulations Jeff Thomson on your 200th no-ball for the season."

Jeff looked fit to murder when it was pointed out to him. He stormed into the dressing-room and grabbed the telephone on the wall. Unfortunately for the scoreboard operator, the S.C.G. internal phone numbers were taped to the wall.

The one-sided conversation went like this:

"Listen, are you the bleepin' bleep who operates the bleepin big screen? Well, I bleepin' well suppose you bleepin' think you are bleepin' funny putting that bleepin' bleep on the screen. Why don't you bleepin' put some bleepin' thing bleepin' con-bleepin-structive up there or I'll be bleepin' well right bleepin' up there to bleepin' sort you right bleepin' out. Let's see how bleepin' funny you bleepin' well think it bleepin' is when I stick your bleepin' face through the bleepin' screen, you bleepin' bleep!"

As he slammed down the phone someone remarked that if it wasn't for his bleeps, 'Thommo' would be a man of few words.

by
Henry
Blofeld

CALLING THE SHOTS

THE commentary box is as good a source of cricket humour as the dressing rooms or the scene of action out there in the middle. In the 20 years I have sat in front of a microphone I have spent an uncomfortably long time, and with varying degrees of success, trying to suppress helpless giggles which invariably follow when something has been said which has an obvious and none-too-pure double meaning.

Brian Johnston, that modern doyen of BBC cricket commentators, has always been the star in this respect and I shall never forget the chaos he caused in the box at the Oval in August, 1976, when England were being destroyed by the West Indian fast bowlers.

"And I can tell you all at home," he said, "the bowler's Holding, the batsman's Willey."

It was Brian who, in describing the bottom-protruding stance of Hampshire's Henry Horton, wanted to say that he reminded him of someone sitting on a shooting stick. He had three goes at it and got it wrong each time.

Then there was the occasion when a little dachshund ran out on to the pitch at Headingley and Brian said: "He's a splendid little chap wagging his tail like mad. And I can tell you he's a fast bowler because he's got four short legs and his balls swing both ways."

While Brian has been the clown prince in the BBC Test match special team, a series of mostly highly-forgettable puns have continually flowed from his lips.

Other commentators have also had moments of high humour—if in slightly more sedate fashion. John Arlott's description of that first streaker, who appeared at Lord's during the 1975 World Cup Final, was as memorable as it was brilliant.

The young man concerned, a merchant seaman from around the corner in Marylebone, showed a great sense of respect and timing by reserving appearance for the middle of an Arlott spell at the microphone.

He appeared from the grandstand side of the ground, and Arlott takes up the story in his inimitable Hampshire drawl:

"My goodness me, we've got an intruder from underneath Father Time in the person of a strapping young man rippling with muscles. The most remarkable thing about him is that he does not have any clothes on.

"There he goes, striding out towards the middle to what I can only describe as the puzzled delight of a big crowd.

"He's making for the wicket at the Nursery End and umpire Tom Spencer doesn't quite know what to do. Ooh, would you believe it, he jumps the stumps! But all's well, umpire Spencer hasn't signalled 'one short.'

"And now the amply proportioned young man goes galloping away towards the Mound Stand with his arms outstretched, showing 25,000 people something they've never seen before.

"And now a young copper comes across and spoils it all. He's taken off his helmet, placed it over the

offending weapon and now he leads the young man off the field to a night in the cells and a visit to the Marylebone Magistrates Court in the morning."

Thus departed the game's first streaker, little knowing that he had been dignified in such splendid fashion. He had done it for a bet with a nice sense of the occasion and, I dare say, a slight smile.

The Magistrate wagged his finger at him next morning and fined him his winnings. But what a precedent he set, for now we are about 3,285 streakers later, and what a pain they have become.

There was Rex Alston, who got into an hysterical tangle at Lord's in 1954, with the pronunciation of a Pakistani named Afaq Ahmed which, if you think about it, is something of a commentator's nightmare.

Rex was also on the air locally in Port-of-Spain in 1959–60 when the Test erupted into a riot and the crowd began to throw bottles and seats on to the ground.

In those days, the commentary box at Port-of-Spain was old and rather fragile and, as usual, all the spectators were listening to their transistors at full throttle. Rex's sense of fair play was somewhat outraged by the crowd's behaviour and he became a trifle indignant.

"I've never seen anything like it in my life," he said. "The crowd away to my right are behaving like a lot of hooligans. I've never seen such disgraceful behaviour on a cricket ground." And on he went in the same vein. The crowd heard every word of it on their transistors and turned on the commentary box as one man.

In about 30 seconds it had been reduced to a pile of rubble as Rex and his fellow commentators fled for their lives.

One of my favourite commentary box stories happened at the Melbourne Cricket Ground in 1984–85. Melbourne radio station 3AW was doing ball-by-ball commentaries on all the international matches with the redoubtable Harry Bietzel—'The Big H', as he is known in football circles—at the helm. Harry had decided it would be a good idea to do something a bit different and devised what became known as 'clock cricket'.

He and his team didn't bother to describe the normal

field placings like cover point and mid-wicket and extra cover, but divided the ground up into segments like a clock. A ball driven to extra cover was hit to two o'clock and wide mid-on was half past ten at night. It was a novel idea which certainly made an impact even if, with most people, it compounded confusion.

One afternoon, Harry was in particularly vibrant form at the microphone when a batsman drove a ball powerfully and was brilliantly caught at mid-off. 'The Big H' went into ecstacies about the bewildering catch and took a moment or two to decide whether it had been held at a quarter to or a quarter past one. Then he passed back to the studio for a news bulletin. The announcer in the studio took up the story:

"First we must thank Harry for the great description of that terrific catch at a quarter past one. And now I'm going to read you the deep fine-leg news."

The biggest on-air bloomer I have made to date was perpetrated at Edgbaston in 1986 when England were playing India. England were batting and had made their usual good start, losing both Graham Gooch and Bill Athey in the first over before a run had been scored.

Left-handers, David Gower and Mark Benson now began to rebuild the innings and by the time I was halfway through my first spell of commentary, after play had been going on for about 50 minutes, England had reached 30.

I said, "I can tell listeners at home that after that disastrous start, England are righting the ship."

The switchboard at the BBC was immediately jammed with irate listeners demanding to know why a commentator had the effrontery to say that England were right in the shit.

You can't win them all.

by
Bill Lawry

(UN) RUFFLED RICH

THE old saying that "you don't really know anyone until you've lived with him" certainly applies to overseas cricket tourists. You learn very quickly that players you have admired, or maybe disliked, as opponents in the domestic competition are totally different people when you're thrust together in a tour situation.

By tradition, Victorians have never had any great love for New South Welshmen, and vice-versa. I don't have to tell you that the feeling goes way back before my senior playing days, but as a kid I'd sit at the M.C.G. feeling sorry for Victoria and myself as Ray Lindwall, Keith Miller and Alan Walker gave us some terrible pastings. By the time I was selected to play for my State, there was a strong, inbuilt desire to succeed and help crush the enemy from the north.

My first Victorian captain was Neil Harvey, an inspirational leader who rather strengthened my anti-NSW sentiments by moving to Sydney for business reasons and becoming one of the sworn foe. When I was first chosen to play for Australia, it was to tour England under Richie Benaud, who had just completed a successful and exciting series against Frank Worrell's West Indies.

"Another bloody New South Welshman," I thought. I had great respect for Benaud the cricketer. I wondered how I would find him as a man. He was, after all, from the wrong side of the border.

On that 1961 tour, I was selected as the third opener to Bob Simpson and Colin McDonald and was looking forward to a learning experience, to watching at close quarters the greats . . . Harvey, Alan Davidson, Peter Burge, Benaud, Norm O'Neill, McDonald, Simpson.

The Himlaya took 21 days to reach England, but it didn't take me nearly that long to learn that Richie Benaud—whether it be a casual afternoon at the pool or a black tie cocktail party with the ship's captain—was always immaculate. Dressed to perfection. Not a hair out of place. He spoke so slowly and deliberately that everyone hung on his next word. There was no doubt that our skipper was in control of every situation.

I also learned that he was always late. If it were an official function, the team would arrive on time, at 7.00pm, and Benaud would make his appearance at 7.15pm. The team bus would be full and ready to leave for the ground at 9.15am and Benaud would arrive at 9.20am.

I could not understand why a man so professional in all other considerations was never on time. It annoyed me a little. It was frustrating for the newcomers to be there on the appointed dot and watch the captain, as if by plan, arrive late, like a movie star at a premiere or a bride at a society wedding.

As I became a permanent member of the Australian side, I enjoyed Richie Benaud's inspirational captaincy and I enjoyed the company of the senior players, yes, even the New South Welshmen. And learned a lot. But I could never accept that the captain was always late and holding us up. It all came to a head on the first morning of the Third Test against England at the Sydney Cricket Ground in 1962-63.

I was always keen to get to the nets early, have a good knock and plenty of throwing and catching practice. As an opening batsman, it was important to me psychologically to be padded up early and relaxed when the umpires went out on to the field.

We had completed our warm up and practice this day, showered and were almost ready to go when someone realised our captain was not among us. He had not, in fact, arrived at the ground. There was minor panic and just as Neil Harvey was about to go out and substitute at the tossing of the coin, Richie burst into the dressing rooms. He was in a foul mood, cursing Sydney traffic for his lateness.

By the time he had made it out to the centre to toss, I had decided this had become too much.

Now it's one thing to take action and another to take the blame for the action taken. I looked around for a 'fall guy' and standing right there was N.S.W. fast bowler Frank Misson. Frank is one of the greatest guys to have played for Australia, a fine athlete and a team man who loved a laugh almost as much as he loved his cricket.

At lunch I took Frank aside and suggested we had to do something to teach the late Mr. Benaud a lesson. Frank was never averse to a little practical joking but, being a New South Welshman and intelligent as well, he was not about to become involved in anything that might make the captain of Australia look a goose.

Okay, I said, it was just a thought. I had noticed some tradesmen doing repairs in the Members' Bar and during the tea adjournment I borrowed a couple of three inch nails and a hammer. Then I told, individually, my teammates (two notable exceptions, of course) that Frank Misson was going to fix Richie up after stumps and they'd better be around when the captain was getting dressed.

Just before stumps, I nailed Richie's brand-new shoes to the dressing room floor, replaced his socks in his shoes . . . and waited.

It was amazing how long the captain took to shower and dry himself that night. There was the application of a liberal quantity of baby powder and eventually on went the underpants. Then he went to the shower area to comb his hair, team-mates shuffling in that general direction. At last he returned to continue dressing.

The shirt was next, each button painstakingly put into place. The tie took an eternity. First of all it was given a good shake; then, observed furtively from behind lockers or a glass of beer, the knot was tied.

The trousers were more straight forward, as trousers often are. Still it took some time. The creases were thoroughly checked out and a couple of minute particles of fluff plucked and despatched.

At last the socks were removed from the shoes, turned inside out, shaken and placed over the foot—but only after each toe was examined as if it might have a flaw. Then the big moment. The silence was eerie.

Benaud bent down, almost in slow motion, took one shoe in his right hand and tried to lift it from the floor. It refused to budge. He glanced quickly about him, as if to see if he was being watched, and gave the shoe a vigorous tug. No go.

By this time, the other players were reading newspapers, hiding around corners . . . doing anything

not to be seen to be seeing. Richie gave the shoe an almighty wrench. Then he stood up, stretched that famous lower lip to the limit and roared: "BLOODY MISSON."

The dressing room erupted in mirth. Poor Frank—poor innocent Frank—blushed, blinked and tried to salvage something from the situation I'd put him in by helping Richie prise his shoes from the floorboards.

Richie Benaud is still late for his appointments, but I think it was a great relief for all of us to see our impeccable leader frustrated to the point of losing his cool.

Apart from leaving him with a hole in his nice new shoes, it did Richie no harm at all. And Frank Misson and I still get a big laugh out of it 25 years later.

NEVER STUMPED FOR WORDS

WISDEN, the cricketers' bible, does not record the first class debut of Raymond Clarence Jordon. It is a pity, because anyone who saw it will assure you it was an episode which does not deserve to be lost in antiquity. I deem it quite a privilege to do my bit for its preservation.

Ray Jordon was known in district cricket in Melbourne as an aggressive, over-confident, loud-mouthed footballer who had kept wickets for Richmond as a youth and moved on to the powerful Carlton club. He made a name for himself there by keeping excellently to an attack which, at best, was fast to fast-medium.

Jordon loved to stump batsmen by standing up to the medium-pacers. It enhanced his reputation as a Carlton lair. When he was selected to play for Victoria, his keeping and his behaviour were both to be under close scrutiny.

Victorian captain Colin McDonald gave Jordon a warm welcome to the State team and wished him well for the game against Western Australia at the Melbourne Cricket Ground. The big-talking newcomer should have realised it was going to be a pretty fiery baptism because he would be keeping to Australia's fastest bowler of the time, left-hander Ian Meckiff. Jordon had heard a lot about the pace of this fellow but had never actually seen him because of Meckiff's heavy Test commitments.

W.A. batted first and as the Victorians settled in the field, Jordon paced out 15 yards from the stumps, his normal position for keeping to the benign pace of Carlton 'quick' Barney Jones.

Meckiff bowled his first delivery to dour W.A. left-hander Laurie Sawle. It was down the leg side and before Jordon could even blink, the ball had thudded into the sightscreen for four byes.

Jordon, a little paler, moved back five yards and was a picture of concentration as Meckiff thundered in for the second ball. The result was the same although, in all fairness, it must be said that our keeper was partly out of his crouch by the time the pickets rang to the tune of four more byes.

Jordon was angry now. He moved back to the 22 yard mark and waited for the third delivery and, to his credit, was halfway to being upright when the ball hit the fence for byes No. 9, 10, 11 and 12 collectively.

"Surely this is some kind of record," said Neil Crompton at third slip. "Keep this up and they'll declare by tea!" snapped Jack Potter in the gully. Mercifully for Jordon, Sawle was able to put a bat to the remaining balls of the over.

Several overs later, Sawle was facing Allan Connolly.

He got a thick edge and the ball went straight through to Jordon. The slips cordon of McDonald, Lawry, Crompton and Potter shouted for the catch—which was a waste of time because Jordon was on his hands and knees looking for the ball which he had cleanly dropped.

The parochial crowd had suffered enough and a big lad bellowed from the outer: "Where did you get this bastard, McDonald??"

I think we had all—and I include the lad in the outer— underestimated Raymond Clarence Jordon, if not his keeping ability then his resilience under fire. The stocky little fellow turned to the slips cordon and said: "What a debut! The first three balls go for 12 byes, I drop my first catch in first-class cricket—and on the same day I'm told my Mum and Dad were never married!"

Victorians have never laughed very much on the cricket field. They have always taken the game very seriously and I suppose I was generally regarded as being somewhat more serious than most. But Ray Jordon broke us up that day. And how did he take the reaction? Like a Carlton lair, of course.

When Victoria batted, Jordon got his opportunity late on Saturday when we were 6/360. He was out first ball, caught at slip off Ray Strauss.

Past Victorian players have an annual reunion and towards the end of the evening, Jordon always recalls the day he stumped Ian and Greg Chappell off Allan Connolly at Adelaide Oval. They were both magnificent leg-side stumpings.

But every head will be shaken and someone will inevitably reply: "Anyone can stump a Chappell—but tell us about the day you broke the record at the M.C.G.!'

by
David
Gower

FLANNELLED FOOLS

TOO many people nowadays complain that the fun has gone out of the game of cricket, especially at top level, and that there are no characters left in the game. Unfortunately we cannot invite the entire cricketing public on guided tours through the dressing rooms all year round, even as a gesture to help correct this misunderstanding which is probably just as well when we consider the foibles and habits of the average professional cricketer, especially the ones which emerge under pressure situations such as 'Rain Stopped Play'.

At Leicestershire we have a dressing room that comprises players from all social levels. If I say that Les Taylor, who made a couple of appearances against Australia in the 1985 Ashes series and took the final wicket of that series, comes from the lowest stratum, it is not a mark of disrespect or snobbiness, merely a reflection of the fact that for some years before joining the club he was in the employ of the National Coal Board and spent much of his time working deep underground.

What is more his playing companions are likely to be Peter Willey, still playing first class cricket 20 or so years after his debut and a product of the dour North East, Philip Whitticase, chirpy young wicketkeeper from the Birmingham area, and Jon Agnew, often overlooked England bowler whose father farms turkeys just outside this, the fox hunting county, and who sent his son to acquire the benefit of a private education at Uppingham School.

This is certainly not a stockbrokers' convention nor a working men's club, simply a collection of cricketers coping with a tedious delay. They may not take their cards as seriously as the likes of Doug Walters, but they seem to enjoy both playing, and the arguments which are part and parcel of the contest.

As regards an average England dressing-room over the last few years, the mere presence of either I. T. Botham or A. J. Lamb is evidence of character. As far as other occupants of those quarters are concerned, life is far easier when both are fully involved on the field of play; rule one is get out of the way if rain stops play and 'Both' decides he is bored. This is when newspapers tend suddenly to catch fire and simple relaxation is out of the question.

'Lambie' once last year left the umpires locked in their quarters when they were under the impression they should have been at least making their way out to officiate in the afternoon session.

Now, lest anyone should be worried that my definition of 'character' revolves around petty arson and illegal incarceration, I think the way those two gentlemen (I'm sorry if I use the term loosely) play the game of cricket is more substantial evidence as to their true character. It is safe to say that Australian fans have seen more than enough evidence of their relative cricketing skills.

How does one assess character in any case? Most of the stories which surround the likes of Fred Trueman

42

appear to be fictitious, though they have provided him and many others with plenty of ammunition for after-dinner speaking and have all become accepted as legend.

For myself I can confess to having been educated in professional cricketing terms by another hard ex-Yorkshire professional, one Raymond Illingworth, again a man not unknown to Australia. He, as my first professional captain, had a proper job on hand in trying to turn me from a complete amateur into some sort of professional cricketer, starting with my appearance off the field.

My turning up at Trent Bridge one day with one black and one brown shoe, hastily donned in the dark before setting out from Leicester, was not his idea of off-the-field discipline. I tried to atone for this casual error on our next away trip which took us down to the town of Taunton in Somerset. After a very average Saturday, I attempted to impress my captain at breakfast on Sunday by arriving in full dinner suit complete with an identical pair of gleaming black shoes.

Ignoring all this and also the unusual occurrence that I had even made it to breakfast at all, Raymond was totally deadpan in his response: "Ah, just got in have you?"

Possibly more embarrassing, certainly at the time, was a small misunderstanding, this time on the field of play. We gave a particularly unprofessional performance one Sunday afternoon in Essex, where most of us at some stage dropped catches wherever we had been placed in the outfield, and lost easily to the home side, prompting a nasting rash of fielding practice sessions during spare moments through the following week, with the aim of rebuilding our confidence under the high ball.

Our next Sunday match was at home to Derbyshire on a rare day—bright blue skies and burning sun (remember this is England we are talking about).

When Raymond came to bowl his allotted spell in the Derbyshire innings the crease was occupied by Ashley Harvey-Walker, one not prone to blocking offspinners, and I was again sent out to graze in the pastures at deep mid-wicket, where shortly after, the hoped-for chance arrived, hanging many a mile up in that blue sky and apparently not intending to come down for quite a while!

When it did, and mercifully stuck in the hands fate had decided would catch it—mine, as no-one else's seemed close enough—I decided to celebrate in time honoured fashion and threw it high into the air. Instead of the expected acclaim, all I got for my trouble was a loud cry in unmistakable Yorkshire tones along the lines of "throw it back, you daft bugger, it's a no-ball!"

Now the ball seemed a very long time in coming

down while the Derbyshire batsmen decided to run their second. When my throw eventually rifled in—yes, those were the days—and hit the stumps at the bowler's end, the richotet once more took it away from my colleagues in the field, so the batsmen, though almost helpless by now, again forced themselves to run!

Three off a no-ball—I wondered why Raymond did not look too pleased!

by
Geoff Lawson

GOB STOPPER

DESPITE predictions that they would take years to cover the retirement of Andy Roberts and Joel Garner, the West Indies managed a quality multi-pronged pace attack for their 1988–89 tour of Australia. But don't they always? I regard myself as something of an expert on the ferocity of this attack because a particularly nasty delivery from Curtly Ambrose broke my jaw in five places during the Perth Test.

A lot of people took my injury quite seriously, but not so our own fast bowler, 'Swervin' Mervyn Hughes.

After a night in hospital, my mouth rendered immobile by what seemed to be several metres of wire, I returned to the W.A.C.A. ground about lunch time in case the state of the game demanded that I bat in the second innings. There are those who say I am not a pretty sight at the best of times and the severe swelling and bruising to the left side of my face must have made me look grotesque. The lads were concerned about my health, but Merv decided I had earned a new nickname: I was 'Mumbles' for the rest of the match.

Merv is particularly fond of his tucker and I was surprised by his absence at the tea adjournment that day. He returned just before play resumed and handed me a small, gift-wrapped parcel. "A gift," he said, "for the infirm."

I was quite touched. What a nice thought from the big, ugly bugger. An early Christmas present to ease my pain.

I ripped the parcel open, hoping for a book or maybe even a video. No, nothing like that. A box of spearmint chewing gum!

A MAD DOG'S BREAKFAST

CRICKET tours to the sub-continent are a lot of things, but never dull. They are particularly interesting when you have a character like Ian 'Mad Dog' Callen aboard, as Australia did on the 1982 trip to Pakistan.

Ian, the Victorian quick, played only one Test in his career, taking six wickets against India at the Adelaide Oval in 1977–78. His nickname was derived partly from his attitude towards batsmen and partly from his off-field behaviour. He was renowned for his impressions, particularly of the Great Ape. His 'alligator sliding into a swimming pool' was also a joy to behold, as was the 'trout catching a fly' as he emerged. A man of many talents.

A six-week tour of Pakistan always seemed much longer and this one must have seemed more like six years to Ian, whose cricket was restricted to just one match by a series of obligatory stomach upsets.

By the time we reached Lahore for the final Test,

Ian was well aware that the safest thing to order for breakfast was eggs, toast and coffee. It wasn't a particularly sustaining meal, but at least you weren't risking another bout of dysentery. Ordering even such simple fare was a bit of a project, a combination of pidgin English and sign language and no matter how well you got your message across, the result was still likely to be a fiasco.

Breakfast would often arrive 45 minutes after the order, and in any sequence at all. The coffee may be served first, followed by the toast, then the eggs as a 'dessert', but after five days of such pot luck at our Lahore hotel, 'Mad Dog' decided he would put the house in order.

On the sixth morning he collared the waiter he had nicknamed 'Manuel' and laid down the law. He was prepared to make concession on the toast, but "bugger it all, Manuel, the eggs and coffee *must* be served together. Savvy." Manuel pondered the instruction, did an excellent impersonation of his 'Fawlty Towers' namesake, blinked, nodded and said: "No worry, Midder 'Mad Dog.' You are my favourite cricketer and I do as you command. I bring eggs and coffee together."

And he scurried off to the kitchen.

The other guys in the dining room had watched Ian's performance with much interest and a lot of them drifted over to our table to await the arrival of a rare synchronised breakfast.

'Manuel' reappeared several minutes later, cup of steaming coffee in hand. He set it down before his favourite cricketer, broke the shells of the two raw eggs and emptied the contents into the cup. "See, Midder Callen," he said, with a 'delighted-to-oblige' smile as wide as Sydney heads, "eggs and coffee come together!"

"YOU ARE MY FAVORITE CRICKETER — EGGS AND COFFEE TOGETHER IT IS !"

by
Allan
Lamb

A Man of Steel

WHEN my Northamptonshire colleague David Steel was
selected to play for England for the first time, one writer
memorably described him as "everyone's idea of a bank
clerk who went to war". Steely was 36-years-old at
the time and the wisdom of sending in a newcomer
of that age against the ferocity of Dennis Lillee and
Jeff Thomson was widely questioned.

David had waited a long long time to represent his
country and his debut was further delayed when he
got lost on his way out to bat. Instead of going down
two flights of stairs and out through the Lord's Long
Room, he went down one flight too many and finished
up in the basement. There he met a guy in a white
coat. Steely thought he was an umpire, but he was,
in fact, a lavatory attendant. "Sorry Mr. Steel, you've
come to the wrong place," he said.

When he eventually found his way out to the middle,
a reception committee was waiting. David was an odd
sight with his grey hair sticking out from under his
peaked cap, his steel-rimmed glasses and his Groucho
Marx walk. When he got to the crease, Rod Marsh
turned to Dennis Lillee and said: "Hey, what's your
Dad doing out here?"

Normally nothing upset Steely, but after he'd been

50

there for an hour-and-a-half and was really beginning to flow with about six runs to his name, and Marshy was still chirping away about his age, he really did blow his top.

"Hey Marshy," he said turning round to his tormentor, "have you seen this?"

"What's that?" said Marsh.

"This arse," said Steely. "You're going to see it for a bloody long time!"

And he did. Steely batted for hour after hour in the last three Tests and finished with 365 runs at an average of over 60.

THE HARRY LIME THEME

CRICKET for me has always been about enjoying oneself and having fun. I have never been able to bring myself to believe that the game should be played with a straight bat and a frown. The attitude goes all the way back to my days as a teenager in the Western Province side under the captaincy of Eddie Barlow.

Now Eddie was a very dominating figure. He led from the front, inspired by example and if nothing was happening, he was the man who made things happen. As youngsters, we were pretty scared of him.

That didn't stop me having fun, though, and it was while I was being punished for a prank during a match against Rhodesia in Salisbury that I discovered belligerent Barlow had a sense of humour after all.

Eddie had me paying for my indescretion that day

having me alternate between third man boundaries. It's a damn long walk and by the umpteenth time I'd made the trek at the end of an over I was getting more than a little fed up. I mean, I was young and fit. I didn't need the exercise.

I was standing there silently cursing the skipper when I noticed a bloke with a bicycle just beyond the

boundary. Egged on by Brian Davison, who played for Rhodesia in those days and who happened to be standing near the perimeter of the arena, I persuaded the bloke to lend me his bike.

He must have wondered what the hell I had in mind, but at the end of the over I cycled straight across the pitch on my way to my far-flung outpost.

I thought I was going to be in for the biggest rollicking of my life, but everyone—Eddie included—saw the funny side. When the mirth had subsided, Eddie shook his head and, still grinning broadly said: "Okay. That's it. You can forget about third man."

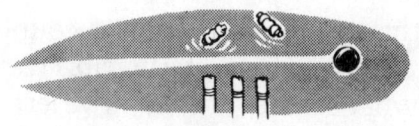

DRIP-DRY DEREK

DEREK Randall has been a constant source of amusement to me since I moved to England in 1978. We've shared a lot of hilarious times on tour, and the incident which always springs first to mind is the bath that went wrong at the Town House in Adelaide during our Ashes campaign.

I was sharing a room with Derek and I left him one evening playing taped music and running a bath while I went down to the bar. Just after I'd left, and before he got into the bath, Derek heard (or believed he heard) a knock on the door. He was wearing only a towel when he answered it and, finding no-one there, stepped out into the corridor to investigate. As he did, the self-locking door closed firmly behind him.

Meanwhile, down in the bar, a group of us were

sitting around having a beer and chatting with the hotel manager when he was approached by a concerned assistant. "Sir," he said, "we have a bit of a problem. We've just had to move some guests in the restaurant because the ceiling is leaking on their table."

At that moment, in walked Derek. Now if anyone else had walked into the bar of this plush hotel wearing only a towel, it would have created enormous interest. But knowing Derek as we did it barely raised an eyebrow.

"What's up?" we asked. "I've been locked out of the bloody room, mate," he said, "and I haven't got a key to get back in."

Derek felt the top of his head as a couple of drops of water fell from the ceiling. The horrible truth dawned on him. "And what's more," he said, "I've left the bloody bath running!"

I still marvel at the good nature of the hotel manager as he and his staff went about the mopping-up operation. Still, how could you be angry with the comical, scantily-clad figure of Derek Randall standing there offering apologies?

MY AFRIKAAN OATH

AS a South African playing for England, I was supposed to know all about Kepler Wessels, a South African playing for Australia, when he made his Ashes debut in Brisbane in 1983-84. Every bowler in our team asked me the same question: "You know him well enough—

how does this Wessels play?" My answer was that in South Africa, we'd got him out on the 'out'. "If you bowl just outside off stump, we'll probably get him caught in the gully," I said.

I went very close to being recognised as some sort of tactical genius because Ian Botham put one right on the suggested spot early in Kepler's innings and he duly despatched it in the air, and at a rate of knots, in my direction at gully. I dived and fleetingly held the ball, only to spill it as my hand hit the deck.

It was to be a very costly miss for England because Kepler dug in. He decided one chance was going to be all England would be allowed. As his score mounted and he defied our every effort to dislodge him, Ian Botham took me aside. "What do you say to this guy to upset him?" he asked. "He won't say a bloody word!"

I told 'Both' every Afrikaans swearword I could think of and each time he was within earshot of Wessels he gave him a mouthful. Kepler was unmoved..

He was not moved, in fact, until he made 162. Later, in the Australian dressing-room, 'Both' approached him. "You know what Lamby's been telling me to say to you, don't you?" he said. "Yes," Kepler replied, "just about every swearword in the Afrikaans language."

"Well, it must have affected you," Ian said.

"Oh Yes," Kepler assured him. "It encouraged me to play better than ever."

It was suggested later that I could have made a fortune as a reverse psychologist.

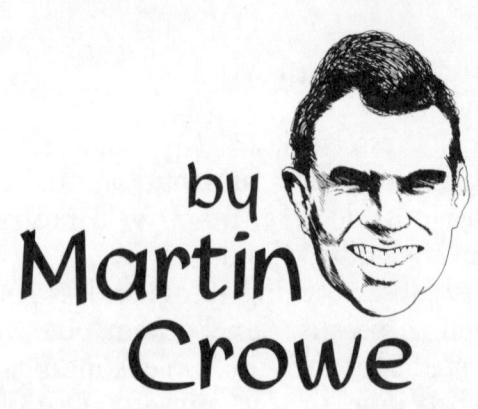

by
Martin
Crowe

LORD OF THE LOB

WE Crowes, brother Jeff and I, have mostly nurtured our sporting reputations on the world's cricket fields, but, like all sportsmen we are fascinated by the mysteries of other games. We find the subtleties of tennis particularly offer the ultimate challenge.

As kids, Jeff and I once played each other in the junior championship final at the Piha Beach Club. I was eight, and Jeff, a sapling of 12. The crowd saw a memorable match in which service was held only once, but that was enough for Jeff to scrape in 9–7.

Many, many years later our father was on the receiving end of a tennis smash from Jeff not long after we had returned from a West Indies tour. The ball had to be levered out of the netting behind the court by two men after it had screamed past Dad's head and lodged in the wire mesh. "That's what it was like in the West Indies," cried 'The Chopper', "every ball!"

'The Chopper' was the sinister sobriquet Jeff had earned during a professional cricketing, and social tennis stint, with David Hookes in South Australia.

At Hookesy's Tennis Finishing School, Jeff would have absorbed the very best in up-market sporting psychology, as well as phraseology. 'The Chopper' euphemism implied the education was a success.

My game, on the other hand, tends towards the more sensitive, the touch game that betrays a sense of subtlety. I mention all this by way of introduction to one of the most outstanding tennis tournaments of all time—the Colombo Classic, 1984.

Then, the New Zealand cricket team was in Sri Lanka for our first Test series against that country. Travelling with the team was Ron Brierley, now Sir Ron, businessman and cricket enthusiast.

Incredibly, while he was watching and talking cricket in Sri Lanka, his business organisation was putting together the largest single financing deal ever conducted by a New Zealand company group at that time.

When challenged about his absence from the negotiations to follow a cricket tour, Ron replied: "Well, I got my priorities right, didn't I?" It was this same sharp focus which Ron Brierley brought to bear when he joined me in the Colombo Classic.

My heart had sunk when the pairings were announced for I could not see how a combination involving Brierley R. and Crowe M. would be any match for such a big gun team as Crowe J. and Boock H., for example.

We would find out. Came finals day and they were our opponents. Tactics had been fairly well sorted out in the preliminary rounds.

Heather Boock's reputation as a wife and mother was clearly out of the top drawer, but her tennis game remained of the dark horse variety.

'The Chopper', having played so much with Hookesy and being unable to avoid a certain rub-off, used speed and strength tactics to carry the team. He would simply call on Heather to serve ("anywhere, just get it in then get off the court"). The same theory applied to the return of service: get it back and he would do the rest.

Ron and I saw our tactics as more of a team effort, with me tending the net while Ron roamed the baseline. In the earlier rounds this had worked well, for many of the opposition's returns were weak enough for me to exercise the smash.

If the ball did clear me first time, then Ron would invariably lob the ball back to set up my next kill.

Now the final. And Ron, with the same dedication which marked his corporate raiding, applied his winning tennis formula mercilessly, and constantly.

Each time the ball came over the net, almost always from 'The Chopper's' racquet, and, mostly on a good length, Ron would pound it high into the air with his version of attacking play—the lob.

On, and on, would go the rallies—with Heather waiting politely at the court's edge. We piled on the

points. Umpire Jeremy Coney suggested I would be welcome to use a chair at the net if I wished. 'The Chopper' was finding it difficult to contain his frustration. Heather was finding it difficult to conceal a giggle.

And Ron was playing the lob, secure in the knowledge that its deployment would bring him the ultimate sporting accolade—victory!

Shirtless, but fully equipped with headband, sweatbands and wristbands, 'Ron The Lob' seized every chance to towel down between lobs. Or to change his racquet grip, anything to slow down the play.

It was a re-run of that celebrated match between Stephen Potter and Joad C. when the former coined the term gamesmanship to mark his dominance over the philosopher Joad.

In his immortal work, "The Art of Gamesmanship", Potter suggests to his students that a fruitful early ploy in a tennis game is to hit a return of service high to the top of the court's wire mesh surrounds, and then to mildly inquire whether the shot was out?

Ron's way varied only in that he would lob the ball high into the murk and haze of the late afternoon Lankan sun, and, aided by the slow court surface, ensure that most of the sting was taken from 'The Chopper's' increasingly furious returns.

It was inevitable. 'The Chopper' was tamed. The old bull had triumphed over the young. Cunning and craft had tossed the block-bash mentality of the Hookesy Tennis Finishing School.

Arise Sir Ron! The knighthood wasn't officially announced until 1988 and then for services to business management and to the community. But those of us in Colombo that steamy day in 1984 know better!

by
Rod
Marsh

WALL TO WALL FETTUCINE

BELIEVE it or not, Bill Lawry and Tony Greig are great mates. And, having spent a few seasons commentating with them, I like to think they are both mates of mine.

You may cast your minds back to the 1970-71 season and wonder how Bill and I could be friends. Didn't he declare on me when I was 92 not out at the M.C.G. in my first Test? Sure, he did. But to forgive is sublime (or so I'm told).

In Tony's case, any harsh words we exchanged were in the heat of a Test match and are long forgotten. They were, in fact, forgotten shortly after 6.00pm on the day, when the tops came off a couple of blizzardly cold beers.

Quite often during a series these days, Bill, Tony and I dine out together. Ian Chappell often joins us— and has even been known to sit next to Greigy. Just once each season, all the commentators dine together. It happens in Adelaide, and there is a very good reason for the congregation. Senior commentator Richie Benaud is guest chef for a mutual friend, Graham Ferrett, at his popular restaurant Ferrett's Place. Proceeds from the evening go to the Primary Club for handicapped children.

Graham has a long history of looking after cricketers

when they visit the City of Churches. He used to be in the car game and before the days of fringe benefits tax, a car was a very handy commodity because every cent you saved on taxi fares increased your chances of being able to quench your thirst.

The 1987–88 nosh-up at Ferrett's Place was on a Friday night during a game against New Zealand. The commentators, with the exception of chef Benaud, assembled in the foyer of our hotel to be driven to the restaurant by Greigy. Of course. Why 'of course'? Simple really. Tony is a great believer in the four c's— cricket, chardonnay, children and cars. No way does he ever let anyone else drive.

I throw the 'children' on to that list because Tony's son Mark, then 12 was in town for the Test and was sharing a room with his Dad. He wasn't invited to the restaurant and I think it's fair to say that room-service (unlimited) and in-house videos would appeal to the average 12-year-old far more than Richie Benaud's cooking. That is merely an observation, not a criticism of Richie's culinary talents.

Lunch is taken at 1.00pm during a Test match so by 7.45pm, when we arrived at Ferrett's Place, we were peckish, to say the least. But socialising had to be done before we ate. We couldn't really expect food too soon anyway because Richie had arrived in the kitchen only half an hour earlier.

The place was packed with old friends from the cricketing and general sporting world of Adelaide. The champagne was flowing freely and Bill Lawry—a teatotaller—made a dreadful mistake. He had a drink. Maybe it was the big-boobed waitress who enticed the 'Phantom' into a glass of the demon bubbly. I don't know, but one glass led to four or five.

Bill then compounded his mistake by sitting next to Greigy at the table. Tony showed no mercy, pumping chardonnay into the now-glowing Bill at a rate of knots. Come 11.30pm, when the last strands of the Benaud fettucine had been swallowed, and it was up and off home for a very unsteady former Australian opener. Or was it? No, not quite.

Tony was clearly delighted with the job he had done on Bill, and he wasn't finished yet.

I'd been observing the performance while quietly sipping on a black duck and when Tony whipped the cork from a bottle of sauterne—at Ferrett's insistence— I had a feeling I could be needed. The man's a maniac near wine. He drinks it so quickly. But I reckoned it was a celebration of his night's achievement in getting Bill very, very pissed.

After another hour or so—and much more wine— Tony made a quite astonishing request: "Morshy, can you please drive the core home? I don't think I could get it out of the core pork." He needn't have worried. Thanks to an early-departing teatotaller, the car was now safely back at the hotel.

There is not a nice way to describe the end of the evening. Tony got to his hotel room after bouncing off walls for the length of the corridor. He was led to bed by young Mark. Bloody difficult getting a key into a strange lock, or any lock, when you're legless, to which I think most of us can testify.

Then there's that nauseating sensation when you lie on your back, fully clothed, and the stupid bed takes off. It wouldn't be so bad if it flew around the room in a regular flight pattern. You guessed it: Tony threw the famous Benaud fettucine everywhere, all over the room.

Now poor Mark being an obedient lad, had to clean it up, and probably would have done so without any prompting if he wanted to get any sleep at all.

Meanwhile, a couple of floors below, Bill Lawry was paying a similarly-heavy price for his evening of uncharacteristic excesses. The difference between Bill and Tony was that the 'Phantom' had no-one to clean up after him.

Mark Greig was up bright and early the next morning and met Bill in the lift on the way down to the foyer. "Good morning, Mr. Lawry. How are you today," he said.

"Mmmm. .Mmmm. . .not very well, thanks Mark," Bill replied.

"Oh," said Mark, "Did you eat some of Mr. Benaud's fettucine as well?"

INVERTED LOGIC

FOR an Australian cricketer, an Ashes tour is obviously the ultimate. I was lucky enough to have four, each a marvellous experience, each with its special and memorable moments. I intended that my last trip to England would be on semi-active service, as a number two wicket-keeper. I envisaged my golf handicap going down to something like brother Graham would regard as "reasonable for a scrubber". And I was prepared to accept the extended waistline which would be an inevitable consequence of part-time work. It didn't work out that way.

Let me take you back to the 1977 tour, which was probably the least rewarding of all.

I was a selector on that trip and I figured I had it made. As a selector I could virtually nominate the games in which I wanted to play. Assuming you performed well in the matches leading up to the First Test you and your fellow-selectors couldn't leave you out of that team. And provided you did okay in the First Test you were a moral for the Second . . . and so on.

Australia always took 17 players on tour and demanded that the full squad be present only at the Tests and the one-day Internationals. It meant that if you were a selector and played your cards right you could dodge a lot of county fixtures (at which a muster of only 13 was required) and have a bit of a paid touring holiday at the expense of what was then known as the Australian Cricket Board of Control.

Being a fair man, I thought it only correct that the number two wicket-keeper in the '77 squad, Richie Robinson, be given every chance to perform. Consequently he played many county games. It seemed rather pointless that I should be 12th or 13th man, except for the odd occasion. What I'm trying to say is I had a fair amount of time off, particularly in the lead-up to the First Test.

Although not a tour selector, Doug Walters, was the senior player and, being very close to the number one wicket-keeper, meant that he had a considerable amount of time away from the team. I know what you're thinking: Marsh and Walters away from the team together, playing golf during the day and drinking all night. Well you're wrong. The team management was too smart for that.

They arranged so whenever Dougie had a game off

I didn't—and no matter how hard I worked on the other selectors I could never swing them around.

It reached the ridiculous situation of Doug and I not seeing each other for a full two weeks. When we eventually met up the night before the game against Somerset in Bath we had a lot to talk about.

As luck would have it we were staying in one of those hotels where if you're a house guest, you can drink all night. This was never the intention, but, as I said, we had many things to discuss, considering the team management had kept us apart for a fortnight.

I can tell you that Walters and Marsh were pretty hung-over during the first day's play against Somerset, so come lunchtime, after being in the field for the first session, all we wanted to do was rest. But there was none of that.

There is another cute little custom about playing cricket for Australia in England. Because of the testimonial and benefit system in county cricket, there is one member of every county side, who, each tour, asks the Australian captain if his players would mind signing about a thousand autographs so that he can flog them, make a quid and basically be well-heeled when his playing days are over.

I have never known a player to get a knock back from any touring team. The autographs which bring the most rewards are those signed on a cricket bat.

At auction or raffle, a bat with the Australian touring team autographs can bring the beneficiary anything up to 1000 quid. So obviously he is going to get as many bats signed as he can.

In addition to having to sign at every county in the country, there are thousands of kids at every Test and county match who keep scrap books. Now these kids may have 100 photos of say, Greg Chappell and they expect every one signed. And then there are the team autograph sheets. We are required to do 10,000 of these.

They come in books of 30 and during my first tour, in 1972, little Dougie Walters taught me a short-cut. You signed only the top four or five and the four or five bottom because these were the pages the manager would mostly check. Well he saved me a lot of time, did Doug. Mind you he owed me a lot considering all those hours he kept me at the bar.

So there we were at Bath cricket ground, hungover and in need of rest, and the 12th man started producing these bloody books. And after the books came the bats for someone's benefit.

It was accepted policy that if you were going to do the bats you may as well do them properly because you were helping a fellow cricketer. And when Doug came across a bat signed upside-down by Len Pascoe, he had a few words to say.

"Lennie, you bloody idiot, you've signed this one the wrong way up!"

"Jeez, Freddy," said Len, "how'd you know it was me that did it?"

by Viv Richards

A MATTER OF RECORD

I'VE managed to make the cricket section of the Guinness Book of Records with one or two performances I've had over the years, but my most unusual claim so far hasn't been noticed.

I reckon I'm the only cricketer ever to have batted *officially* three times in a match—and still not scored a run!

It happened when I was playing in the Leeward Islands tournament back in 1969. I was still at school, an 18-year-old, to whom playing for Antigua meant everything. Test cricket was still a long way in the future and that, to me, was then my Test match—especially as it was against our arch-rivals St. Kitts. The feeling between the two islands, separated by only 100 miles or so of the Caribbean, is like that between Victoria and New South Wales, or Yorkshire and Lancashire, and, in those days, the atmosphere was not far from Test cricket, with noisy crowds of over 5,000 each day.

I was a bit of a darling of the Antiguans, being a schoolboy and all that, and they were looking forward to me doing well in that particular match at the Antigua Recreation Ground. So they weren't too happy when I was out fourth ball for 0. I was even less happy since the umpire ruled it was a bat-pad catch. I knew I hadn't touched it and it wasn't difficult to detect my mood when I walked off.

I was fuming, the crowd was fuming and, before you knew it, they had halted the match, shouting: "No, Vivi, no match!" There was a lot of pallaver between the officials as all this was going on and they eventually bowed to the crowd.

I was astonished when someone came and told me I could bat again and a fresh-faced 18-year-old doesn't need any encouragement to bat, so out I went. Once more, I was out quickly, this time no argument, stumped by a long way. Again for 0.

What with all the confusion and talk, I was determined to make up for things in the second innings—but it didn't work out that way, I was out for 0 again, my third of the match.

Guinness Book of Records, please copy!

NICE ONE, LENNIE

ON one of my early tours of Australia, we were discussing fast bowlers, as batsmen so often do, when Ian Chappell made a comment I've never forgotten. "They're really only bullies," he said, meaning that most of them couldn't take as good as they got.

It's all very well sitting around chatting to say how you should, or shouldn't deal with a bowler hurling it down at 90 mph and out to do you serious physical damage. It's another getting out there in the middle and doing it.

Yet I think I can safely say that I enjoy the confrontation with a fast bowler doing his best to get me in every way he knows how. It may well be that

I have the same type of aggressive mentality. And there's always a great feeling of satisfaction, almost superiority, when you can get the better of a tearaway pacer.

Now they don't come much more tearaway than Lennie Pascoe, who I first came across in World Series Cricket. No one was more aggressive, or tried harder than big Lennie. And he loved bowling bouncers.

When I came out to bat in the second innings of the last Test of the 1979 series at the Adelaide Oval, Lennie had just got Desmond Haynes caught behind and was all fired up. He let me have five bouncers straight up and, as I ducked under each one, he came snarling up the pitch with some comment, such as, "if you cop one of those, it's the hospital, matey"— or words to that effect.

All the time, he was wasting energy and when he did pitch one up, it turned out to be a fairly gentle half-volley. When I hit it back past him, I knew it was four from the time it left the bat, even with the long Adelaide Oval straight boundary. But I wanted to get close to him to see the look on his face and give him one of my own. Just to let him know who was boss, you understand! So even though I knew the ball would reach the boundary, I ran all the way down the pitch as if I was taking runs. I didn't intend saying anything, but I knew he mightn't have been too keen to even get a glimpse of me just then.

Well, I ran past the crease, past the stumps and still further as he was walking back to his bowling mark. I never did get close enough to him to look him in the eye.

I was a little cheeky, a little arrogant, call it what you will. But it's not often you can get your own back on fast bowlers and it's nice to savour the moment!

COOL HAND LANCE

MY first tour of Australia, in 1975, was a disastrous one for the West Indies. Australia had a very strong side with the Chappell brothers and Ian Redpath always among the runs, and Dennis Lillee and Jeff Thomson at their peak, backed by Max Walker and Gary Gilmour.

We were struggling and, not for the first time with a touring team, the umpiring was beginning to get to us. We were sure we were getting the dirty end of the stick but Lance Gibbs, the senior player on the trip, kept telling us to keep our cool.

"I've been here before on two tours, I know the place well," he would keep saying. "They'll try and rattle you with anything. Just don't fall into the trap. Keep calm and cool."

It was very good advice and, like all the other young first-timers in the team, I was intent on following it. It was only that Lance himself, who played his cricket as hard as anyone I've seen, found it impossible to follow his own advice.

He'd had a few appeals turned down by Jack Collins in the Melbourne Test and you could see the steam coming out of his ears with every one. When he had one lbw against Redpath rejected, it was the last straw.

He snatched his white hat from Jack Collins and stomped into the outfield. When he came back for the next over, he was still simmering. Collins put his hand out to take his hat, as is the custom, but our senior player, who had kept hammering into us to "keep cool", deliberately refused to give it over.

Instead, he stuffed it into the back of his trousers and bowled with it there. We didn't hear too much about cooling it after that!

by
Ian
Wooldridge

THE DOWN UNDER DUKE

ON a late summer's afternoon in 1962, in the august environs of the Committee Room at Lord's Cricket Ground in London, a joke backfired with such magnitude that it was surprising no vast mushroom-shaped cloud formed above the building. The extraordinary thing is that its victim never knew it was a joke until the day he died, 13 years later, and, to this moment, not more than a handful of confidantes are aware of the bizarre events that day.

The England cricket team to embark for Australia a few weeks later almost picked itself. The hang-up was Item Three on the agenda, who was to captain it?

There was much discussion about a young man of lordly countenance and enormous talent for the game. Name of E. R. Dexter, amazing striker of the ball, terrific golfer, latter-day Corinthian, public school and Cambridge, blue blood wife. But also, in the eyes of some, arrogant, difficult, loftily indifferent to either diplomacy or the problems of the professionals, fiercely independent.

"Look," said one of the company, "we all know Ted Dexter can handle a bat, but the point is who can handle Ted Dexter? "

"I can," interrupted a richly plummy voice from the end of the table.

At which every eye turned upon a somewhat squat man with a deeply florid complexion.

For a start no-one knew what Bernard Marmaduke Fitzalan-Howard, K.G., P.C., G.C.V.O., G.B.E., T.D., 16th Duke of Norfolk and Earl Marshal of all England, was even doing at the meeting. True, he was a well-known cricket nut with his own private ground down at Arundel in Sussex, where visiting international teams traditionally started their tours. True, he had been President of the Sussex County Cricket Club as early as 1933. True, he had been president of M.C.C. in 1955. But his fame now came from stage-managing all the great State occasions: Coronations, Royal funerals and weddings, farewells to the great warriors of the Land. He was, probably, the courtier closest to the Queen, upon whom he was in almost daily attendance.

"I can," repeated the 16th Duke of Norfolk. "Dexter is a first class young man for whom I have the most enormous respect."

"In that case," laughed the man who had questioned Dexter's qualities of diplomatic leadership, "you'd better go to Australia as team manager."

"Just a moment," replied the Duke. He rose, walked with his slow and stately gait to a sideboard telephone, asked for a line and dialled a Sussex number. It was answered by Lavinia, Duchess of Norfolk, his wife and mother of his four daughters. "Darling," he said—for the British upper classes can be quite sentimental—"Do you mind if I go down to Australia for five months this winter?"

No-one could catch the Duchess's reply.

The Duke resumed his seat at the table and announced: "Yes, that will be in order."

A few weeks later the England cricket team flew from London to Aden, there to board the liner, Canberra for Fremantle, Australia. Ted Dexter was captain. And Bernard Marmaduke, Duke of Norfolk, was manager.

The small moral to this story is that you should never jest with the British Establishment. They've usually had the last laugh since Henry VIII burned down the monasteries. And, for all the jibes about Hooray Henrydom and in-breeding, they do have a considerable talent for organisation. The Duke of Norfolk, in fact, was a raving success.

There were many jokes within the joke, mostly involving the manager's conscientious determination to become one of a touring party, if not exactly one of the lads.

On our second night at sea he decided to get to know the press. The invitations were formally printed and delivered to our cabins. Black tie, of course, 7.15pm for 7.30pm dinner in a private apartment. There was some amusement at the parsimonious 15 minutes allotted for pre-table drinking. We were yet to learn that the Duke was not exactly averse to a decent cocktail or five, but this was the breaking-in period.

On the stroke of 7.30pm we sat down. To make us feel utterly at home the Duke did not delay his few remarks until after dinner. He rose immediately and delivered two immortal sentences.

"Gentlemen," he said, "I want this to be a completely informal tour. You will merely address me as 'Sir'."

It sounds ridiculously pompous but wasn't. For almost all his life he had been surrounded by people addressing him as 'Your Grace'. What he was actually asking was virtually his idea of calling him 'mate'. Everyone relaxed. He revealed a brilliant dry wit and there was established that evening a rapport which lasted, for most involved, for many years.

He did not at first, find Australian egalitarianism easy to cope with. He told us a glorious story one evening of, for him, the probably unique experience of having to hail a taxi in the street. It was in Perth and the driver derived from somewhere in Central Europe.

The cab pulled into the kerb and, with uncommon courtesy, the driver reached across and opened the door. It was, naturally, the *front* door. It may be taken as read that the Duke of Norfolk had never travelled in a front passenger seat in his life.

"Excellent man," reported the Duke. "Not ungiven to garrulity, but extremely friendly. Asked me what I was doing in Australia. I told him. Asked me what my name was. I told him I was the Duke of Norfolk. He became rather excited. "Does that mean that you are related to Duke Ellington?"

Bernard Marmaduke chuckled about that over several brandies. He was not the bribing type, of course, but when his ship came in he was extremely generous. His wine merchants in London had been ordered to deliver a certain brand of Scotch whisky to appropriate Australian venues and on several occasions a bottle would be delivered to one's room with a scrawled note that hoped you were enjoying the tour.

During the Western Australian leg of the tour we popped over to Kalgoorlie for a match. I do not now remember the name of the hotel at which we stayed but I have a vague recollection that it wasn't the Ritz or Claridge's. There appeared to be one bathroom, set back from a wrought iron balcony, for about 30 residents on the upper and only other floor.

His Grace appeared in royal blue dressing gown, clutching toothbrush and razor. He joined a lengthy queue. No-one stood aside. Players and pressmen engaged him in conversation while he waited his turn. There was neither rudeness nor grovelling sycophancy. He had to stand there with the rest.

There was also in Kalgoorlie an evening in Paddy Hannan's Club. His Grace, at one stage, found himself almost pinned between a slot machine and two gentlemen, informally attired, who were giving their considered opinions about everything from Gallipoli to the proposed European Economic Community which would certainly not do the Australian economy much good.

From time to time hoping his gestures passed unnoticed the manager rolled his eyes at would-be rescuers among the English party. None would rescue him. It was that evening's joke. And it was that evening he did, unknowlingly, become one of the boys.

He escaped eventually and simply said, "Phew!" We loved him for it. There were times he became irascible but, then, who doesn't on a long and demanding tour? We learned a great deal from him but there is no doubt that he learned a great deal more from us. It was interesting that as the tour progressed he mostly chose as his partner for the Sunday golf matches one Freddie Trueman, a Yorkshireman who had battered his way from mean streets and coal mines to the top in cricket. They became genuine friends and Freddie, not the most discreet of men in most relationships, has never breathed a word about the confidences they exchanged. Such was his respect for the manager who, in your terms and mine, had conned his way on to the trip.

On that tour England were fairly lucky to get away with a draw in the First Test in Brisbane. Ted Dexter, with 70 in the first innings, and 99 in the second, led from the front.

The Second Test in Melbourne was a different story. England won. But not without a managerial trauma.

Ken Barrington, the colour sergeant of the batting

line, was out of sorts. He scored an unconvincing 35 in the first innings and was worried about his form. As precise a man who has ever played Test cricket, he was invariably in bed by 10.30 pm during a Test. So imagine one's surprise on returning to the Windsor Hotel from some foray or other around one am, strolling into the lounge for a final night-cap and finding Barrington hunched morosely over a glass of whisky that looked mahogany in colour.

Obviously there was some tragedy at home. Clearly a close relative or the family dog had died. What was it?

"Can't sleep," moaned Ken. "Went to bed early. Tossed and turned. Wide awake. Came down for a scotch to see if that will do any good. I'm going back to bed now to see if it works."

It didn't. The most meticulous and orderly man had worked himself into such a state of agitation that sleep was impossible. So he tried a desperate measure. Aware that the ducal manager was a near insomniac who relied on heavy sleeping tablets for a few hours rest, he telephoned the Duke of Norfolk's room.

An age passed before the phone was answered. "Yes?" demanded a gruff, disgruntled voice.

"I'm sorry about this, sir," said Barrington. "I wouldn't do if it weren't vital. The fact is I just can't sleep. Playing tomorrow and it's all going round and round in my mind. Do you think I could possibly come down to your room and get a couple of those tablet bombs of yours?"

"All right," growled the Duke, realising that, after all, this was part of a team manager's duties, "come down right away."

Barrington replaced his telephone. As he did so he

fell back on his pillows and lapsed into an exhausted sleep.

Below him, the Duke of Norfolk, wide awake himself, now waited. And waited. And waited. But Barrington never came. The Duke never slept another wink that night, Barrington slept through till breakfast, like a baby.

I was not present when the two men met the following morning. But it is reliably reported that a haggard looking Duke, on passing the great English batsman, simply said, "Damn you, Barrington." It became a legendary story when England won. I heard the Duke tell it against himself on several subsequent occasions.

Unhappily, neither man is here to tell it yet again.

There was only one discordant note on the Duke of Norfolk's one and only managerial assignment.

Shortly before Christmas on the tour an official announcement to the press revealed that the Duke would be returning to Britain for a few days. Several Australian newspapers, and one or two British ones as well, were outraged. Here was typical Establishment privilege at work. The great man went home for Christmas with his family while the troops stayed in some far-flung field.

The Duke went home and returned some ten days later to face a really hostile press conference in Adelaide. He said little, taking the criticism on the chin. Then he retired to bed, visibly hurt.

Some nights later he asked a number of us to his room for a late-night drink. He had something to tell us, he said, that we must pledge never to write until his death. We gave our word.

"The reason, and the only reason, for my return to

England," said the Earl Marshal of British ceremonial, "was that I was commanded to do so by the Queen. She informed me that Sir Winston Churchill was failing in health and I was to prepare for his State funeral. This I did."

On several of those freezing mornings back in Britain he orchestrated the great British regiments through the streets of London, preparing for what Churchill wanted as his departure from this earth—the most spectacular funeral ever granted to a non-Royal. And that, rightly was what he received in due course.

In retrospect, therefore, I shall never forget his reply to an Australian journalist's question at that Adelaide Press conference. "But what did you *do* when you were back in England?" demanded the reporter.

"Oh," replied the Duke of Norfolk. "I saw the Duchess and I fed the ducks."

The Test series was drawn and Australia retained the Ashes. The Duke protected Ted Dexter's shoulder blades, as he said he would. On one occasion the Duke received an agitated telegram from Lord's in London demanding to know what course of action he was going to take about one of Dexter's commercial ventures which was receiving unfavourable publicity in London.

The Duke's reply was thus:

"Don't bother us. We are trying to win a cricket match."

The complex joke was certainly on Lord's that day. His Grace the 16th Duke of Norfolk may not have been the greatest team manager ever to bring English cricketers to Australia. But as man he never had a rival.

by
Richard
Hadlee

SKINNED!

IN India the crowds can be a bit unnerving. Boundary fielders have copped the odd bit of fruit and veg behind the ear.

My brother Dayle figured in an extraordinary incident when New Zealand played Pakistan at Dacca in 1969. Kiwi opening batsman Bruce Murray—known as 'Bags' because he was B. A. G. Murray—was down on the third man boundary feeling like he was the target in a coconut shy. He complained to captain Graham Dowling who told him to stop the game if anything else came his way from over the fence.

Not long after a fast-moving banana got 'Bags' fair in the back of the neck. He picked it up and ran towards the pitch, brandishing it as if it were a Man of the Match cheque! Dayle was on his way in to bowl and quite oblivious of Graham Dowling telling him to stop because 'Bags' was on the move. Dayle let the batsman, Asif, have a short riser which was fended into the vacant gully area.

Well, it had been vacant before 'Bags' took off on his fruit delivery run from the boundary. He arrived just in time to take an outstanding diving catch, coming up with the ball in one hand and the banana in the other. The umpire called 'dead ball'.

82

HAPPINESS IS A DRY FART

WHEN survivors of cricket tours to the Indian subcontinent get together it's inevitable that much of the chat will be about the most basic bodily function.

This is because a large part of a tour of India is spent either on the toilet, or trying desperately to get there before it's too late.

In India is a species of water snake whose bite causes death within nine seconds. The great England fast bowler Fred Trueman claimed that after he'd been in India for three weeks he went looking for it.

I had such a dreadful time with my health on the 1975-76 tour of Pakistan that I was most reluctant to tour there again, and in fact didn't take part in the 1987 World Cup in India and Pakistan for that very reason.

But the prospect of becoming the greatest wicket-taker in the history of Test cricket, and assurances from all quarters that conditions in India had improved out of all recognition, persuaded me to take part in New Zealand's tour there late in 1988.

But had things changed? Well, yes . . . some of the hotels we stayed in were magnificent as was the hospitality showered upon us; and, no . . . there was no escaping the dreaded 'Delhi Belly'. At one stage, during the First Test at Bangalore, we were so short of fit players we had to draft in Ken Nicholson, a reporter with Television New Zealand, and former New Zealand captain Jeremy Coney, who was in India as a radio commentator.

Coney said later that when he was fielding in the covers he looked around the rest of the field and realised there wasn't one player on the offside who had been selected for the game!

Surely clear enough proof of the truth of that old saying: in India, happiness is a dry fart.

In India, after you've had the runs for a while, you learn to walk around with your buttocks clamped together. New Zealand's opening bowler Ewen Chatfield tried to do just that, and, at the same time drop the ball on the spot.

It is normal practice on the field that as the bowler runs in 'the field' walks in with him, watching him at the moment of delivery, then switching concentration to the batsman. Something was wrong! There was a sort of 'oooh' from the crowd.

Attention switched back to 'Charlie' Chatfield. The ball had not been delivered. It was still firmly in place in his hand. 'Charlie' had run through the crease and was still running . . . past the startled batsman, past the keeper and the slips, past fine leg and on up into the dressing sheds, an ominous shadow spreading over the seat of his creams.

EYE IN THE SKY

ON our plane trip to Australia for the 1980–81 tour Jeremy Coney donned an air hostess's uniform. He played out the part perfectly, even down to graphic displays of how to best utilise the sick bags. One New Zealander player summoned hostess Jeremy and ordered a drink for himself and . . . "one for my snake". The player had the notorious one-eyed trouser snake draped impressively over a cushion on his lap! Hostess Jeremy returned with a glass of neat vodka which he splashed in 'the snake's' eye. The creature kept a droopier profile for the rest of the flight. And the tour!

"IT'S GOOD TO SEE YOUNG CHARLIE GETTING THE RUNS!"

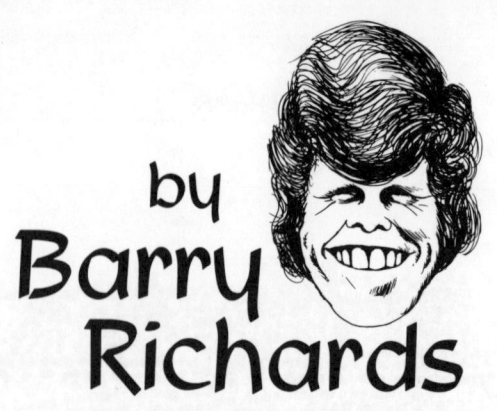

by Barry Richards

MISTER ROBERTS, SIR!

ONE of the highlights of my 11 years of English county cricket with Hampshire was to see at first hand the emergence of one of the greatest fast bowlers the world has seen. Andy Roberts.

Andy took more than 100 wickets in his first season with Hampshire. He also "took" more than a few for the other bowlers, whose life was made easier by batsmen desperate to grab a few runs before being blitzed by the West Indian demon.

During my second season with the county, the Indians were touring England and Andy's reputation had spread like wildfire throughout the cricketing world. It had certainly not escaped the attention of the Indians, whom we met an hour before the start of the traditional tour fixture at Hampshire. And it had made a particular impression on one of their number.

This little fellow moved along the line introducing himself and, in accordance with Indian custom, addressing the opposite number by surname: "Hullo Richards . . . hullo Greenidge . . . hello Sainsbury . . ."

It went like that until he reached Andy. There was reverence in the Indian's eyes as he looked up at the imposing West Indian and said: "Hullo, MISTER Roberts."

IN BLACK AND WHITE

KERRY Packer's World Series Cricket was a revelation to the South Africans who had never been allowed to play at Test level. To the couple of us who had, it was a joy to return to that standard of competition.

Rivalry between the W.S.C. teams was intense, but humour abounded and there was always going to be something ironical with the West Indian—South African scenario. That irony was brought home to me in a taxi I shared with two West Indian players after a night game in Melbourne.

I sat in front, Bernard Julian and Joel Garner in the back. The driver was curious about my accent and asked me where I was from. "South Africa," I replied. "Oh," he said, and lapsed into several minutes silence.

I noticed him glance several times in the rear-vision mirror at the two black guys in the back. Eventually, he said: "S'pose you're from South Africa too."

After a 10-second pause, one of the back-seat passengers replied: "Man, are you colour blind?"

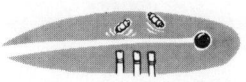

One of the surprises of World Series Cricket, as far as I was concerned, was the obvious ill-feeling between Australian captain Ian Chappell and Tony Greig, who led the World XI.

It seemed to me that the antipathy went a lot deeper and was a lot more personal than the standard rivalry between opposing skippers.

The extent of their mutual dislike became quite evident during a game in Perth. Gordon Greenidge was carrying an injury and called for a runner, a call answered personally by Greig, who had been dismissed cheaply after Dennis Lillee had peppered his early prototype 'motorcycle' helmet with some rearing deliveries.

Chappell certainly didn't want Greig out there running for Greenidge, for the obvious reason that he was captain and would be in the ideal position to personally advise his batsmen. The Australian skipper formally protested to the umpires, who conferred and said, "play on." A seething Chappell retired to first slip to plot his next move.

Two overs later, he approached the umpires again. "Greig cannot act as a runner because he is improperly attired," he told them. "Greenidge is wearing a helmet and Greig is not, and the laws state that the runner and the batsman must be identically attired."

Greig immediately called for his helmet.

"That's impossible," said Rodney Marsh from behind the stumps. "It's been sent downtown to the panel-beaters for repair."

After one particular W.S.C. night game in Melbourne we were having a quiet beer—a lot quieter, certainly, than whatever the young ladies at a table in the hotel lounge had been drinking for what was obviously an hour or three. They must have been celebrating something.

We must have been conspicuous, too. You don't go anywhere with Joel 'Big Bird' Garner—all six foot seven of him—without attracting attention. Eventually, one of the girls approached us. "You're Joel Garner, aren't

"YOU'D BETTER SEND THAT HELMET TO THE PANEL-BEATERS, MATE!"

you?" she asked. "Yes, ma'am," Joel replied with customary courtesy.

"Look," she said, "We've noticed how tall you are. And you have big hands, big feet, long arms, long legs . . . What we're dying to know is, is everything else in proportion?"

"Lady," said 'Big Bird,' "If it was, I'd be eight foot six!"

89

by Sir Garfield Sobers

Now Pull This One!

NYRON Asgarali was a Trinidadian opening batsman who played a couple of Tests for the West Indies on the 1957 tour of England, my first. It was his first as well and it seemed he didn't appreciate the difference in climates between Trinidad and England in May.

One bright, sunny, but distinctly chilly morning, 'Asgar' appeared in the dressing room, beaming all over his face and pronouncing himself "fit as a fiddle and raring to go". Those who knew England well advised him to warm up.

We lost the toss and, as we took the field, 'Asgar' sprinted to his position at fine-leg. It wasn't long before, chasing a ball, he suddenly pulled up and hobbled up to report the bad news to us in the middle.

"But, 'Asgar', I thought you were feeling as fit as a fiddle. Now what's wrong with you?" asked John Goddard, our skipper.

"I've pulled a muscle," came the reply.

"Where?" asked Goddard.

"In both legs," 'Asgar' answered, making his way, very painfully and sheepishly, back to the pavilion.

That's cricket! And because it's a 'funny' game, with some funny expressions, there can often be funny situations. Take the West Indies' tour of England in

1966. Our team then included several players who delighted in practical jokes—Rawle Brancker, Joey Carew, Wes Hall, David Allan, Peter Lashley. Not a day went by but for some prank in the dressing room on some unsuspecting individual.

But not everyone can take a joke and, in any case, some went too far. So I got together with the manager, Jeffrey Stollmeyer, and we decided we would put an end to it. We were well into the meeting, talking things over, when Charlie Griffith arrived. Not clued in on what we were talking about, he jumped up in a flash when I said that there was too much leg-pulling and it really had to stop.

"No more leg pulling?" he asked, his face serious with concern. "Well, how am I going to get any runs then? You know that the pull through leg is one of my best shots. I can't understand it!"

We all burst our laughing—and Griff had his leg pulled about it for weeks afterwards, although he never stopped his favourite pull shot either.

Charlie's fast bowling partner, Wes Hall, is one of the greatest characters I've ever played with. He was a naturally funny man and I reckon he could make you laugh at a funeral without even trying.

But, like all fast bowlers, he took his batting very seriously and, on his day, he was no rabbit. We had a few stands together in our time, none of them very long, but that against England in Port-of-Spain in 1968 was vital to the outcome of the match.

We had followed on just over 200 behind and when David Brown, the big fast bowler, got three wickets in the final over to tea on the last day, we were 180 for eight and in real danger of losing when Wes came out. Now I seldom gave instructions to the batsman at the other end. A word of encouragement to a young player, perhaps, but nothing more. I felt that if he was playing Test cricket he knew his responsibility and Wes had played enough that I was sure he knew his. In any case, there's not too much you can tell a fast bowler about batting!

So I watched in horror from the opposite end when Wes played at the first five deliveries from Brown and missed them all by miles. The ball whizzed past the off-stump, bounced over the middle stump and, somehow, Wes survived the over.

By this time, I felt I had to say something so I went down and said: "Wes, you know you missed those balls by a long way. You're playing down the wrong line."

Without batting an eyelid, he replied: "Oh, I knew I was doing something wrong. Thanks, skip!"

And he didn't do anything wrong after that as we

held out the England bowling, averted defeat and, in the end, when we were safe, Wes even started playing some shots at the leg-spin of Kenny Barrington and Robin Hobbs.

As we walked off after it was all over, I let Wes lead us into the pavilion and, very quickly, the reporters were around us. One asked Wes if he was ever worried out there about the position.

"Worried?No, not personally. My only worry was for the fellow at the other end," he said, pointing to me. Never at a loss for words, Wes.

Wes also happened to be a little absent-minded in the field and, I suppose like most of us, would drift off near the end of a hard day.

This specific hard day was at Leeds in the 1966 Test against England and Bob Barber, the England left-hander, was holding us up as we pressed for victory. Wes was down at deep backward square-leg and, with not much coming his way, his thoughts were somewhere else—Barbados or Newmarket or London but certainly not on the ball that Barber hit in his direction. Suddenly, someone woke him up with a shout of "catch!" but it was too late. The ball went through his hands and caught him a heavy blow on the forehead.

Just as we were moving to see whether he was alright, we saw Wes coming towards us, not rubbing his head but with a pronounced limp!

by
Peter Roebuck

CLOSE ENCOUNTERS OF ANOTHER KIND

EVERY so often cricket throws up a leader of the bulldog variety, a character who storms and curses, charges and barks, sweats and bellows, until finally the battle is won. Whereupon he buys double scotches all round and everything is forgotten—until next morning.

Yorkshire, England and Somerset had one such fellow a few years ago in Brian Close, who looked and played like Winston Churchill in one of his "we'll fight on the beaches" moods.

Close was big, burly and bald. When he wasn't within earshot, Somerset's young pros, a motley crew which included your correspondent, called him "the bald old blighter." He shouted at us, occasionally remembering our names, and generally gave us an upbringing out of the old school.

Close left Yorkshire in high dudgeon, after decades of service, after one of those disputes in which they specialise up there (though later Somerset showed Yorkshire didn't have a patent on them). Determined to carry on playing, he moved to our distant, gentle farming community.

Impulsive and formidable, Close had no intention of fading away. Up north he was used to winning and he intended to carry on, even if it meant upsetting local applecarts, (of which there were plenty, apple cider flavoured by dead rats being the farmers' preferred drink.)

Moreover, Close was a big enough man to stand up to any odds. To him the greater the odds, the greater the challenge. He had an unshakeable faith in his own talents, which included playing golf, left-handed or right-handed.

He wasn't conceited so much as convived. He shook the county into life. When he was about, even the milk carts went smartly about their work.

From the start at Somerset, Close led by example, gritting his teeth, crouching bareheaded at short leg, snapping at recalcitrant fieldsmen and generally storming from dawn until dusk. He was the sort of fellow who, following his instincts, would lead you from the trenches into a hail of gunfire.

Every day brought heroic deeds and horrible mistakes, for which he did not consider himself accountable. In victory, he'd chuckle; in defeat he'd growl about the gods as if they, too, needed bringing into line.

As a man, Close lacked hardly one flaw. Rashness was his enemy. He was the bull in the china shop. Nothing was ever his fault. If he failed it was because of some extraordinary conjunction of events entirely beyond his control: the ball had bounced on the only blade of green grass left on the wicket . . . the 12th man had brought out the wrong chewing gum . . . someone had moved behind the bowler's arm at the moment of delivery (this usually led to him storming off in the direction not of the pavilion, but of the itchy spectator.)

He did not calculate his moves with the care of a chess player. He barged forwards, refused to contemplate even strategic withdrawal, and generally led a life of thrills and spills. Stories about him are legend. You followed him, taking care not to fall behind lest you got a rollicking.

Once at Trent Bridge, he went out to bat with Barry Stead on a hat-trick. Somerset was in trouble but the captain was on the bridge. He swapped observations with the departing crestfallen debutant, the tubby Richard Cooper, who had just gone for a gozzer.

Somerset were 3/42 and the ground was hushed as Close took guard. Fieldsmen huddled around the bat and only Nirmal Nannan was left to patrol the outfield. Somewhat to our surprise, Close had a vast swipe at his first delivery. He was a trifle unlucky. After following a gentle parabola the ball dropped straight into the hands of the solitary outfielder.

The crowd erupted and Somerset's dressing room fell into devastated silence. Close stormed into our near-deserted room, banged his bat on the floor, glared at Cooper and growled: "Bloody hell, lad, you said it were swinging but you never said it were seamin' too."

He was not one to contemplate his navel. Nor did he ever doubt his own talents.

Another time, in Worcester, presented a rare occasion—Roebuck going well, Close struggling. A few overs passed and Close strode down the pitch to his callow partner.

Thinking I was in for a few words of congratulations, I joined my captain mid-pitch. "It's a bloody funny game, lad," he said, "they're bowling right well to me and they're bowling crap to you."

Brian Rose had a similar experience. By chance, Close was dominating the strike in the early overs of the game, so Rose asked him what the bowlers were up to.

"It's shifting all over the place," Close said. "I'll be all right, but you might struggle."

Then there was the Somerset-Nottinghamshire game in Bath. A wicket fell and in walked Sir Garfield Sobers, the greatest cricketer of them all. Wise old pro Tom Cartwright, thousands of wickets to his name, was bowling.

He approached Close, 50 years experience between the pair. Young Somerset cricketers huddled around, eager to discover what subtle play these two giants were contemplating.

They met in the middle of the patch. Close turned to Cartwright and said, as if imparting the secret of the universe, "Now then Tom, this lad's a left-hander." Then he walked away.

Somerset once had a 40-overs game sandwiched in the middle of a Championship match. On the Sunday, Close decided to swipe every ball into an adjoining graveyard, an endeavour in which he was successful for a time. Then he copped one on the mouth, scattering teeth, blood and gum all over the place.

Close reappeared next morning groaning with pain, clutching his swollen jaw. In walked Maurice Hill, who knew nothing of the accident. "By heck, I've got a toothache this morning," Hill said.

Delivered from behind his morning paper, Close's look would have done justice to Bette Davis.

Brian Close was not, of course, a figure of fun— just a brave and uncalculating man of generous disposition to whom things happened. In short, he was accident-prone. Presented with a sponsored car once, he smiled, waved to the cameras, drove out and ran straight into a lorry.

The sponsor hadn't even put away his duster as the crumpled car limped back into the garage. Close, of course, escaped uninjured. He wrote off lots of cars, one being deposited behind a hedge some distance from the road when his concentration was temporarily distracted by a tight finish to a horse race.

Close was indestructible. Once, somewhat in his cups, he walked through a glass door and escaped without a scratch.

He retired in 1977, still cursing, still giggling, glaring and fighting. He returned to Somerset in 1985 to play in a friendly.

On the field he scowled and growled as before, chin jutting out. Last ball of the innings he positioned himself on the boundary and the batsman, one Vivian Richards, skied a catch. Close hovered under the steepler, running first this way and then that. Up and up the ball went and his manoeuvers continued. Nor did they stop as the ball began its descent.

As it dropped, the 54-year-old man staunchly awaited its arrival. Finally it plummeted and crunched into the turf some yards away from where Close had taken up his final position.

For once, we were barely able to hide our laughter. We trooped from the field and sat silently, a tribute to the old days. Close sat down, too, and sipped a stiff scotch.

Eventually, he spoke, "You know it's a funny game, this, lad. I got into the right position but t' bloody ball fell too quickly."

Brian Close was a marvellous fellow to play with or under.

"I GOT IN THE RIGHT POSITION BUT T'BLOODY BALL FELL TOO QUICKLY!"

by **David Hookes**

WILL THE REAL JEFF THOMSON PLEASE STAND UP

CRICKET tours of England are rather notorious for the number of official functions the visitors are obliged to attend. Australia's 1977 Ashes tour was no exception, with something like 13 receptions in London in the first 11 days. The format at each was the same, the players sitting at tables with guests and counting down the time to leave and wander into the Sportsmen's Gambling Club to make their contribution to the British economy.

During each function, captain Greg Chappell would speak on his team's prospects and introduce the players individually. Protocol demanded that when your name was called you stood briefly to let the guests have a look at you.

One of the major functions was held at the Savoy Hotel, where the Duke of Edinburgh headed a star-studded guest list which included Ted Heath (the immediate past Prime Minister) and comedian Eric Morecambe. Len Maddocks, our team manager, told us to be in the foyer of our hotel, the Waldorf, at 7.00 pm. "The team bus will leave for the Savoy at seven sharp," he bellowed as the players dispersed from a Lord's training session for a rare free afternoon.

Jeff Thomson and I had decided to play golf at

Denham Golf Club, about an hour's drive to the north of London. We finished just after six and I said to 'Thommo' that we should be getting back. "Okay," he replied "but we should have a drink with the club captain and the blokes we played with."

After much cajoling, I managed to prise Jeff away from the bar about seven and not even his lead-footed driving could get us through the Friday evening London traffic and back to the Waldorf before eight. A very quick bath (no showers at the Waldorf) meant we arrived at the Savoy at 8.15pm.

The function was for 1600 people and, being so late, we tacked on to the end of the line. Most of the guests were already seated when we got there but 60 or so were still milling around the doorway hoping to catch a glimpse of these Aussie cricketers.

The procedure was that as a player walked through into the reception room, the doorman would ask his name and shout it loud enough for those inside and out to hear. "Introducing Mr. Greg Chappell . . ." and so on. A polite round of applause would follow as the player shook hands with the Duke, Heath and Morecambe.

The word got around that Jeff Thomson had not yet arrived. After what Jeff, in tandem with Dennis Lillee, had done to the Poms in Australia, he was a very big name. He had badly injured his shoulder in the meantime and missed a tour of New Zealand and the Centenary Test.

But with Lillee's withdrawal from this tour, 'Thommo' was to be our frontline strike bowler. All England wanted news on that shoulder. To the Poms, he was the difference between winning and losing the series. Everyone wanted to see this destroyer of batsmen in the flesh.,

I was in front of Jeff as we filed towards the door with the last of the guests. But he had other ideas. He tugged at my blazer and whispered: "Watch me stuff this doorman bloke up." And with that he strode past me.

"Name?" asked the doorman. "David Hookes," said Jeff. He walked through, met the dignitaries and calmly sat down.

I was next and I glanced furtively behind me to see if other people had joined the line, which would have enabled me to sneak back and grab a little breathing space. No such luck. So I took a deep breath and moved on.

"Name?" asked the doorman. "Jeff Thomson," I sheepishly replied. What else could I do. I had no choice. The doorman announced: "Introducing Jeff Thomson!"

I walked through and said hello to the Duke. Ted Heath asked me how my injured shoulder was coming along and Eric Morecambe wished me well in the absence of my partner-in-crime, Dennis Lillee. I said thanks, smiled politely and sat down.

Later in the evening Greg Chappell began his standard routine of introducing the players. He presented Rod Marsh and Doug Walters first, as vice-captain and third selector. They stood up, made only a couple of inane remarks, to Greg's considerable relief, and sat down. The rest of us were then introduced in alphabetical order . . . Ray Bright, Ian Davis, Gary Cosier. Then Greg said: "From South Australia, making his first tour to England with an Australian team, David Hookes!" 'Thommo' and I both stood up.

Greg did a double-take and quickly moved on to Kim Hughes as 800 people looked at Jeff and 800 looked

at me.

After a few more introductions, Greg said: "And making a welcome comeback to the Australian team, possibly the fastest bowler the world has ever seen, Jeff Thomson! No-one stood up.

'Thommo' obviously regarded it as a huge joke and did very well to fight back a fit of the giggles. Greg was not amused. At all.

Neither was Maddocks when he gave us a nice old verbal the next day. We were not allowed to forget the Savoy caper all tour, but it was worth it to have got a grin out of one of those dead-dreary official functions.

A VERY NEAR THING

AT the same time as admitting that I've had my share of run-ins with umpires, let me say that I respect them enormously. I respect anyone prepared to make a career, even a part-time job, of ruling over what goes on out there on the cricket field. It's all flak and no glory. But there are umpires and there are umpires.

A good umpire makes the right decisions almost all the time and is also a 'good bloke'. He accepts, or tolerates, most of the player idiosyncracies and draws the line only when he really must. He doesn't command respect—he gets it automatically.

At the other end of the scale is the bloke who thinks a white coat is the uniform of 'El Supremo'. He's the boss, and you'd better know it! Don't mess with me, boy! You can usually pick this type by the exaggerated flourish of his finger when he says "yea" or of his head when he says "nay". The other giveaway is his compulsion to over-assert his authority by involving himself in things way outside his portfolio.

Such umpires don't make it, thank God, to first-class level. But we had a classic example in district cricket in Adelaide.

Such was this bloke's nature that he actually called West Torrens fast bowler, Dean Smith for throwing. It was quite a shock to everyone, except this officious ump because Dean had won a Bradman Medal for best player in the competition. It indicated that we had quite an extraordinary umpire because he called Dean while standing at the bowler's end!

He was therefore able to pick a flaw in the bowler's arm action and watch his front foot at the same time. Amazing. We'd always been led to believe that "chuckers" were brought undone from square leg.

Ian Edgley is a very prominent lawyer-businessman in Adelaide. He was my captain at West Torrens, and at Thebarton Oval one Saturday afternoon in 1976 he handed me that ball and asked me to send down a couple of overs of my unplayable "Chinamen" to the Port Adelaide tail. My first ball was a classic wrong 'un—or that's my story. Peter Curtain danced down the pitch, missed it by a comfortable margin and was duly stumped by Mick O'Brien.

The umpire so good he could watch a fast bowler's arm and foot at the same time had to get into the act. Couldn't resist it.

As we gathered around the keeper to congratulate him, Edgley picked up the bails and handed them to the extraordinary adjudicator who had flourished the finger at square leg. Instead of rebuilding the stumps, the umpire said: "Mick, you were periously close to taking that ball in front of the stumps."

"You're allowed to," said Edgley.

"You're not," said the ump. The rest of us flinched. We knew 'Edge' was wrong.

Freshly smugged, the goose took on the lawyer: "You are not allowed to," he said, full of confidence.

"Yes you are."

"No you're not"

'Edge' grinned just a little. "You are allowed," he said, "to be periously close to taking a ball in front of the stumps!"

by Ian Botham

CLOSE-UP

FROM the time I first held a bat, people told me there were no characters in cricket any more. But how can that be, when I've rubbed shoulders with so many of them? I can reel off names like Derek Randall, Phil Edmonds, Pat Pocock, Allan Lamb . . . characters all and great value for the spectators when they played for England.

There is no greater character on the current English cricket scene than Dickie Bird, that great umpire and proud Yorkshireman. Dickie can take a joke but is very highly-strung, a trait of which Allan Lamb and I took full advantage during a Test at Edgbaston. We ganged up on Dickie by dropping small crackers which go off when you tread on them into the bowlers' footmark at his end. I actually did the deed while Allan engaged Dickie in conversation for a few moments.

Dickie managed to get back into position behind the stumps without stepping on our bangers, but as Bob Willis thundered in to bowl, off they went like a machinegun. Dickie stepped back to see what was happening and trod on one himself. Being a very jumpy sort of guy at the best of times, he leapt high into the air and came down dancing. All he needed to complete the act were castanets.

Dickie would bring a Test match to a halt by stopping a bowler in his run-up and shouting: "I'm sorry, lads, I've got to go to the toilet. Hang on a minute!" And off he would go. The radio and TV commentators had no idea why he was scurrying from the field. We knew.

But of all the characters in my time, Brian Close was the greatest. Brian was my first captain at Somerset in 1974 and he taught me so much. Most of all, he taught me self-belief. 'Closey' actually believed he was the best cricketer in England, even after he'd passed 40. He once said, in all seriousness, that he could outfight Mohammad Ali. He actually believed, that one lucky punch would be enough, that the best boxer in the world at the time would be unable to stop him.

Brian Close was the fastest and worst driver I have seen. His gambling instincts made him a great captain, although his tips on racehorses were usually a disaster.

He was as hard as nails, the toughest of men. And he taught me never to show pain to the opposition. The bravery of Brian Close was legendary. He was once hit on the temple while fielding at short leg and the ball rebounded to cover for the catch.

As we gathered around him, someone asked what would have happened had the ball hit him between the eyes. "It would have been caught at mid-off," he replied.

And he meant it!

A BIT OF A GIGGLE

CRICKET is at the highest level is, or is supposed to be, a very serious business, but I've never been able to see it quite that way. I suppose my attitude towards the game has been influenced by my charity work for Leukaemia Research. That work has taken me into so many hospitals where I've seen people with just a few weeks to live, still smiling, still convinced that a miracle is just around the corner.

It put things into perspective for me. After experiences like that, how could I regard cricket as anything more than a game? A damned good game to be sure, the best of all games, but a game nonetheless.

I'm glad to say that when I look back over my career, I barely remember one good individual performance from another. What I vividly recall is the fun I've had out of cricket and the great friends I've made. I also remember the draft scrapes I've been in. Sometimes I've gone too far, but I've always tried to keep things in perspective. You're a long time retired and obviously the happiest memories are the ones you want to take with you.

The sense of humour associated with Australian cricket is totally different from the English brand. In Australia they go for one-liners delivered with a serious expression, or for japes like the pig bearing my name which waddled on to the pitch during the Brisbane Test in 1982.

I thought that was very funny and an apt comment on my girth at the time. I blamed it all (my girth, that is) on those lovely Aussie wines and the fantastic Aussie food.

I can think of several po-faced cricketers who would have taken a very dim view of that pig episode had it been directed at them. But I've always believed you have to take it on the chin if you're prepared to hand it out.

I've always told the Aussies that their country is just like their people—big and empty. They know I'm kidding. On and off the field I've had a lot of laughs with the likes of Jeff Thomson, Dennis Lillee, Rod Marsh, Greg Ritchie and Carl Rackemann. They've all agreed with me that although daft things are said in the heat of a battle, a joke is never all that far away.

Did I say cricket was a serious business? England were certainly taking it very seriously at Leeds in 1981 when the Australians had us on the ropes. If I'm to be remembered at all as a cricketer, it will probably be for the innings I played in the second innings of that Test. My 149 not out gave me tremendous pleasure—and for a few reasons. Obviously I was delighted to play a part in turning inevitable defeat into an incredible victory. I was delighted, too, that I was able to play such an innings after I'd been written off by a lot of critics. But what pleased me most is that I got those runs by being relaxed.

I figured that if we were going down, as seemed certain, we would go down with a little flair. I'm sure that if I'd batted like a Geoff Boycott, I'd have been rolled over and England would have lost.

As it was, I spent most of my time out in the middle laughing at the way the Aussie's got more and more upset as my mis-hits cleared the fielders. Luck? Sure, I had plenty of it. I'm not sure about fortune favouring the bold, but it certainly favoured a very relaxed Ian Botham that day.

When Graham Dilley joined me at the fall of the seventh wicket, we were still on a hiding to nothing. I met him as he reached the wicket and said: "You don't want to hang around here for another day, do you Dill? Let's give it some humpty!"

Graham immediately joined in the spirit of the thing and the ball flew to all corners. All the while I was baiting Rod Marsh and Dennis Lillee, who were not amused. I couldn't understand their attitude because Graham and I were thoroughly enjoying ourselves. And I'd always regarded Rod and Dennis as guys with a good sense of humour!

It's a matter of history now that England bowled Australia out for 111 in the second innings and won by 18 runs. The Test has been variously described as "unbelievable" and "the most extraordinary ever played".

To me it was a fun game of cricket.

by
David
Boon

CLOUGH'S COCK-UP

KICK off a cricket trivia quiz with the one about the Australian cricketer who nearly lost the family jewels and all you'd get would be puzzled frowns. Give the answer 'Peter Clough' and you'd get another round of 'Peter Who's'.

Peter Clough was a big, fair-haired, gangly right arm pace bowler who became one of Tasmania's best through sheer persistence and desire. And the day he turned white in the 'Gabba dressing room he became a legend in his own short, cricketing lifetime.

That day was typical Brisbane: warm, humid, the pitch was good, and . . . the Tasmanians were on top of the Maroons! A moment to be savoured.

Test pacemen Jeff Thomson and Carl Rackemann had looked pretty ordinary in the first two sessions. But the banana juice at the tea break worked wonders. 'Thommo' and big Carl came out and bowled the quickest and most menacing spells I have ever faced, including those from the West Indies in 1988-89.

At about 5.30pm Tasmanian skipper, Brian Davison, was dismissed and fast bowler Clough was called upon to do duty as a nightwatchman. Clough had impressed with his willingness to call a spade a spade and an intensity to put his body on the line for the team.

The batting technique of big Pete, who was about 6ft. 6in. tall and most of it legs, was to extend the left foot far down the wicket, and block. Simple.

Against 'Thommo' and Carl it was also hazardous. Clough was hit all over the body. But he gritted his teeth, and batted on. And at stumps when Peter and I left the battlefield it was the lanky paceman who received all the cheers on our return to the dressing room.

Cloughie went to his corner of the room and slowly started to undress. He put down his bat and gloves. He took off his helmet, unbuckled his pads, dropped his trousers and untied his thigh pad. He reached inside his jockstrap to remove his protector . . . the pouch was empty!

Wide-eyed, Cloughie realised he'd been facing Australia's fastest two bowlers without a 'frog'. The dressing room broke up. Cloughie was as white as a sheet.

We duly made our way to the wicket next morning with Cloughie continually giving a little nervous hitch to the groin area. I wondered whether he was checking to see if the family jewels were still there or just checking to see the protector was in fact in place. First ball of the morning was from 'Thommo' to Clough. It hit him in the groin. His protector was split in two!

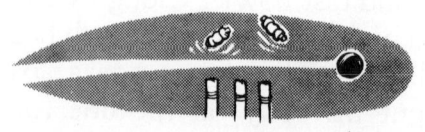

MY MATE 'SWAMPY'

WHEN Geoff Marsh first came into the Test team, cricketers being what they are, he copped a fair bit of ribbing centred about his lifestyle as a farmer at Wandering, a little spot about 60 miles south east of Perth. In amongst all the digs about cocks that crow and being especially nice to the sheep, A.B., the Australian captain Allan Border, was most insistent he knew a bloke from Wandering who must have been a bit of a legend in the town because he was so thick.

Marshy said he didn't know anyone in Wandering who was thick and said A.B. must have been in another town.

"Nope," swore A.B. "He was a farmer, just like you 'Swamp'. And he was sitting in the waiting room at the local hospital, picking the dirt from under his fingernails, waiting for his missus to have a baby."

"So," said 'Swampy', "what's unusual about that?"

"Hang on," said A.B. "When the baby arrived the news was bad. It only weighed a pound. Fair dinkum 'Swamp', the farmer looked up at the matron and said: "That's OK, the bloody drought's been goin' on so long I guess I'm lucky to get me seed back!" And A.B. broke up. My mate 'Swampy' gave him one of those lop-sided grins that says, "I've been had."

'Swampy', tagged with that nickname for only the obvious reason, and I have been tour room mates since the Australian tour to New Zealand in the 80s. I found out 'Swampy' doesn't mind a chat. The boys reckon it's probably because he's not a big reader, farmers being the sorts of blokes who work from dawn to dusk, have a quick bo-peep at the local rag over dinner to see who dipped how many sheep, then go to sleep.

On that Kiwi tour 'Swampy' had celebrated his duty-free status by forking out for one of those huge, ghetto blaster radio things which he nicknamed 'The Gecko'.

During the morning after the first night 'Swampy' awoke, according to the clock, at 5.30am. For me, not a favourite time of day! "Boonie," he asked softly, "are you awake?" "Yes, Swamp," I managed through stiffish lips, a dry mouth and a furry tongue, "what do you want?"

"Do you mind if I turn the music on?"

"No problem 'Swamp'." I dozed off to the gentle sounds of 'The Gecko'.

The alarm clock clattered at 6.00am remember. Again from the direction of 'Swampy': "Boonie, are you awake?"

"Yes, 'Swamp'," I answered, a little testily, "what do you want?"

"Would you mind talking to me, I'm lonely."

The boys call the Western Australian team members the W.A.C.A.s. No wonder! In Bangalore, on a tour to India, I was jet-lagged early on and had some trouble adjusting to the time difference. Fitful sleep was followed by very early awakenings. My idea of a sleeping tablet was a good novel.

So, there I was, propped up in the bed turning the pages of a thriller. 'Swampy', from across the room in his cot: "Do you like to talk, mate?" he asked with that serious 'Swampy' look spreading all over his face.

"Yes, I do mate," I answered in all honesty.

"Well why are you reading that book? Don't you want to talk really?"

"Yes mate, I'll just read a few more pages and then we'll have a chat." I read on but the concentration lapsed because I could sense 'Swampy' getting more and more agitated across the room. Finally ... "Boonie," he growled, "if you read one more page of that book I'm going to tear it up!"

"Yes mate," I said. And kept reading. And reading. Boon went to sleep. Marsh was asleep.

When I came back from breakfast the next morning I looked for my book. I found it in the wastepaper basket, shredded into barely recognisable pieces.

My friendship with 'Swampy' was naturally forged mainly through our successful opening partnership on the field. Before Australia started their series against the West Indies in 1988-89, the Test team sat down on the eve of their first contest in Brisbane. We talked about the West Indians, arguably the best team in the world, fresh from their 4-0 win over England, and about how quick each of their fast bowlers was.

As team vice-captain 'Swampy' had a bit to say: "Everybody knows we're going to get hit at some stage," 'Swamp' said a bit ominously, "but when we do get hit we can't give them the satisfaction of knowing they've hurt us. We've just got to stand there and show no pain."

The next morning 'Swampy' and I made our way to the middle of the 'Gabba. Big Curtly Ambrose was cruising in, bowling his steepling rib-ticklers, Gus Logie was at bat-pad, grinning, and leg slip was around the corner, waiting.

Big Curtly sent down a particularly vicious lifter, but I shouldered arms and let it hit me. Crunch! Right under the rib-cage. I stood there, remembering 'Swampy's' vow, taking extremely deep breaths and grimly gritting my teeth. 'Swampy' came down the pitch. He had a little grin on his face. "It's OK mate, you can give it a little rub." Dry? About as dry as you'd expect from a farmer from Wandering in the middle of a drought!

"IT'S OK, MATE, YOU CAN GIVE IT A LITTLE RUB ...!"

by Richie Benaud

Brandy . . . and Very Dry

RETIREMENT is always a poignant moment. Is one doing the right thing or could you actually play on, if not forever, at least for a season or two, thus proving the slowing of the reflexes is merely an illusion nurtured by some youngster who wants your place in the team. My thoughts were always to embrace retirement earlier than others thought it should happen, hence getting out of the game, from the playing point of view, at the conclusion of the 1964 season at the relatively tender age of 34.

I have never regretted it and have always been grateful that the last summer was a good one, marked at the end by the cocktail party thrown for me by the South Australian Cricket Association at the Adelaide Oval after I made a century there on the final day of the match.

Roy Middleton was president of the S.A.C.A. in those days, he and I had known one another as administrator/player/captain for something like 15 years and he really let himself go in the farewell speech. He had selected as his theme those of us whose names, because of their performances in a walk of life, became so firmly embraced in the minds of the public that it is impossible to forget them.

He talked of the game itself, of Australian cricket, but always came back to the principal theme, that some names will live forever and that it is impossible to forget them.

Then he turned to me, duly embarrassed at this barrage of compliments, and there was a pause. There was a reason for the pause, as I gleaned when I glanced at him, because some of the colour had drained from his face and he was a trifle wild-eyed.

Now I looked with more interest as he said, 'I give you the toast of . . . I give you the toast of . . .'

He had everyone's attention by now as we all waited to hear what was to emerge and it came out as, "I give you the toast of one of Australia's greatest household names . . . Richie Benny!"

He received prolonged applause once everyone recovered from a bout of muscle-draining laughter. The following week, at the Test in Sydney, I walked into the dressing-room to find pinned on the back of the door a newspaper cutting telling of U.S. comedian Jack Benny's impending arrival in Australia.

Alongside, in Sir Donald Bradman's handwriting, were the words, 'Your brother, I presume!'

I resisted the temptation to come out of retirement until I was shanghaied in Kenya in 1979 when the East African team were playing their final trial for the Prudential World Cup in England later in the year.

I was on the trip with the Variety Club, raising funds for crippled children, and a local sports club promised $2,000 if I would umpire the match and another $2,000 if Bobby Charlton would referee a football match.

Everyone was appraised of the fact that all I was able to do was umpire because of degeneration in my back and the fact that the medical men had warned against running even 10 yards, let alone bowling or ducking bumpers. The first thing I saw on stepping off the plane was a newspaper poster, 'Benaud to Play!'

I soon sorted that out with a brisk conversation with the President of the Club and was just turning away when he said gently, "Ah, but the Australian High Commissioner and his wife are great fans of yours and they have already bought tickets and made donations to the charity, on the basis that you will be playing."

Defeat!

It was 38 degrees Celsius, (100 on the old scale), and finally I made it off the field at the end of the match to where my wife Daphne was sitting, rather glumly I thought. "Where's the beer?" I croaked. "It's a dry club," she muttered. It was 38 degrees where she was sitting as well.

When eventually we made it to the home of the President and he poured me a glass of cold ale, I reached for it, my back gave way and I spent the next four days hobbling around Kenya. It remains my final comeback!

On the question of matters not always being as they appear. I know of few better examples than the N.S.W. vs South Australia match at the Sydney Cricket Ground in 1955. The first day was slightly disastrous for N.S.W., with a scoreline of 8/215 late in the day when Keith Miller made one of his surprise declarations. Storm clouds massing behind the pavilion though meant that, much to Miller's annoyance, the umpires allowed an appeal against the light by the batsmen, Les Favell and David Harris, who walked off chortling.

'Nugget' Miller was livid! He still had steam coming out of his ears the next morning when, after a 15 minute delay for a light shower of rain, play began. He took 7/12 and bowled out South Australia, a strong batting side, for 27.

They followed on 20 minutes before lunch and Favell and Harris had added 12 when the interval came, just as two South Australian supporters walked through the turnstiles.

They looked at the scoreboard on the Hill showing 0/12 and one said, "Pretty low scoring." His friend thought for a while. "Don't worry about that, mate," was the reply. "We'll just take our time and make sure of the first innings points against this mob."

There have been many cricketing humorists over the years, players like Bill Lawry, Frank Misson and others, but it was always difficult to beat the deadpan humour of Lindsay Hassett. He was at his very best when confronted with pomposity, and his fun was always gentle, but effective.

The very first meal I had in England in 1953 was at the Park Lane Hotel in Piccadilly where there seemed a slightly supercilious, even pompous, touch to proceedings and, although I didn't know much about service in English hotel dining-rooms, it appeared a little on the tardy side. More waiters than diners, but not a lot happening.

Until, that is, the waiter dropped the plate of ice cream into Lindsay's lap, and the head waiter, eyes raised to the ceiling, murmured something about scooping it out.

Lethargy disappeared the moment Lindsay stood up, removed his trousers, handed them to the head waiter with the straight-faced request that they be returned before he signed the bill and left the restaurant. Two minutes and they were back, clean and dry and the

head waiter's wide, but now not in the least pompous, eyes never left the skipper for the rest of the meal.

He probably felt a little like the society matron in South Africa in 1949 who put on a cocktail party somewhere near Bloemfontein and instructed the team to be there sharp at 6.00pm and wear black tie.

As it was an unofficial function, and they were playing golf prior to the party, they arrived late, already having had an aperitif and dressed in ordinary jackets and ties. She never let up. Strident-voiced and big-noting, she was telling everyone how the greatest vice in the world was unpunctuality, when Lindsay, so the story goes, tossed the brandy balloon from which he was drinking over his shoulder into the fireplace.

In the ensuing silence, he explained deadpan, that it is an old Australian custom, when people are unpunctual, they are expected to show their contriteness by tossing brandy balloons into the fireplace until, in the eyes of the hostess, they have expunged their guilt. For the remainder of the party she kept one hand very firmly on his throwing arm!

by Desmond Haynes

DOUBLE TROUBLE

HOWEVER else it might sometimes seem, umpires are generally pretty good blokes. I think most cricketers appreciate that it's a tough job and I've found that those who have a sense of humour and are relaxed are the best, men like Dickie Bird and David Shepherd, of England, and Lloyd Barker, of the West Indies.

I wouldn't put the Indian, P.D. Reporter, in the same mould. He's more precise and proper—and polite. When the West Indies were in Calcutta on our 1987–88 tour we were staying at the same hotel, and I met him in the lift on New Year's Day. He was very pleasant. "Happy New Year, Desmond," he said, "and all the best wishes!" That's very nice of him, I thought and I returned my compliments for the season.

In the packed Eden Gardens stadium next day Mr. Reporter's finger shot skywards to signal me lbw to Kapil Dev in one of several one-day Internationals we played that season. I wasn't happy.

"Hey didn't you wish me Happy New Year and all the best wishes yesterday?" I muttered as I passed him on the way to the pavilion. "It's not going to be too happy if you keep giving me decisions like that!"

I swear I saw a smile flicker across his stony features as I walked away.

Some of the happiest days I've spent on the cricket field were as a boy in the Barbados Cricket League, the county league in which rivalry between villages and areas was intense. Even if the grounds were small and bumpy, the pitches were usually good and the standard of the cricket always high and intense. It was a tough school and several future Test players came through it.

Each team had its avid supporters—and each team had its umpire. The thinking was that each umpire would be a deterrent to the other "pulling his weight" and it worked pretty well. But exceptions were only to be expected such as the case involving the great West Indian batsman and one of the early heroes, Seymour Nurse.

It happened to be a vital match and Seymour, even at that early age a top batsman, was leading his side to victory almost on his own. The opposing bowlers, were at their wits' end trying to get him out so they approached their umpire at tea and asked for his intervention.

"But you're not even beating the bat, not even hitting the pad," the willing ump replied. "Since you don't look as if you're going to either, here's the plan." And he spelt it out.

On resumption, the spinner tossed one well wide of off-stump, Seymour raised his bat high above his head and let it go through to the 'keeper only to be surprised by a clatter of stumps and bails and a concerted appealing for stumping. He was even more astonished when the umpire raised his finger and exclaimed, almost in triumph: "Out!"

"Out?" asked Seymour. "Out how?"

"Stumped, of course," came the reply.

"But I can't be. Look my back foot is still firmly grounded," Seymour pleaded.

"Oh well, up here we play *both* feet in the crease!" the crafty ump grinned.

QUICK SHAKES

NERVES hit Vanburn Holder, the big Barbadian fast bowler who played for West Indies in the 1970s, in a big way when he came into the Barbados team for the first time as a boy of 19. He was almost unknown since he was playing in the Barbados Cricket League at the time. He felt pretty good when given the new ball, ran up smoothly and delivered the first ball with no problem—or so he thought.

It was only when he noticed the batsman hadn't played a shot or the keeper collected the ball that he realised something was up. What was up was that he still had the ball in his grasp, frozen there by the fear of his first big occasion.

The big occasions once got to Tony Gray, too.

The West Indies tour to Pakistan in 1986-87 was the first for the tall fast bowler and he seemed to fit into Test cricket very comfortably. However, the last Test of the three we played was a real nail-biter and it tested everyone's nerve. They had won the first, we had won the second so this was the decider.

There was only one run in it on the first innings (240 to us, 239 to them) and we really struggled to hold on in the second innings. I managed to stick while wickets fell at the other end and was 88 when Gray came in at the fall of the eighth wicket near the end of the fourth day. We were 212 on and, as I discovered afterwards, there was a lot of discussion in the dressing-room advising Tony as to what to do, and to tell me, when he came out.

As he walked to the wicket, he veered towards me. I waited to hear what the instructions were. I waited . . . and waited. But while Tony's mouth was moving, nothing was coming out! It might have been the heat and the dust but I have a feeling his state had something to do with that terrible phenomenon that overcomes us all at some time . . . nerves!

I was in and well set and I believe, thinking pretty clearly so I tried to calm him down, telling him there was nothing to worry about. "Just hold on!" I said.

He did—for six balls. Then Imran bowled him and Courtney Walsh with successive balls to end the innings and I was still 88 and the score was still 211. The match was drawn with Pakistan holding on grimly— and that was enough for Tony Gray to quickly get his voice back.

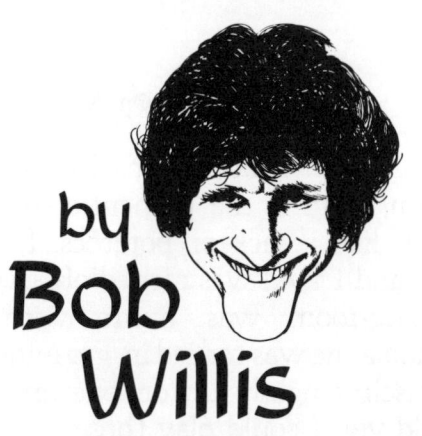

by
Bob
Willis

OINK OINK

IN the heat of Test combat, the funniest things happen
to help diffuse the tension. In 1982, I was taking part
in a desperate last-wicket stand with Bob Taylor to
give us a decent lead against the Pakistanis at Edgbaston
when we walked out after the tea interval. We had
only gone a few yards and I wondered why everyone
was laughing. Then it dawned on me—I had forgotten
to bring out my bat!

That same year, a pig brought the house down during
the Brisbane Test. Someone smuggled it into the ground
and, in honour of our two more corpulent teammates,
the words 'Hemmings' and 'Botham' were daubed on
either side of the pig. Now Ian Botham thought it was
hilarious, but Eddie Hemmings took it rather personally.
His humour was not improved when he drove some
of us rather slowly back to the hotel at close of play.
Graeme Fowler, bored at the slow driving, piped up
from the back seat, "Come on Eddie, put your trotter
on the gas!"

Perhaps the bravest piece of humour in my time came
in the Perth Test of 1974. Dennis Lillee and Jeff
Thomson were at their most frightening on the fast
Perth track and David Lloyd, our opening batsman, was
resolutely getting into line and stoically taking all the

knocks. Finally a vicious nip-backer from 'Thommo' trapped him right in the unmentionables and David went down like a sack of potatoes. It made all our eyes water and David was carried off in great distress. The dressing-room was numb with shock and apprehension as he was carried in, groaning. Then David forced himself gingerly up on one arm and croaked to us, "Told you I could play those bastards with my cock!"

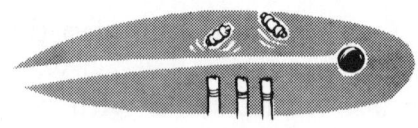

CHEERS FROM BAY 13

DESPITE outward appearances, I did manage to enjoy a few laughs during my cricket career. I know I often looked in a dream world and that I gave the impression the game was very hard work (true! true!) but I put that down to the fact I had to concentrate furiously to give of my best. Luckily I managed a few good performances against Australia because of that fierce concentration but, along the way, there were also some hilarious moments.

On my first England tour to Australia in 1970/71, I encountered that special brand of humour beloved of the inmates of Bay 13 at the Melbourne Cricket Ground. "Hey Willis!" came the cry, "you take ugly pills. In fact you're hooked on them!" One day, in a spirit of Anglo-Australian friendship, I gratefully accepted a can of lager to slake my thirst. Just before I raised it to my lips, I noticed a warm, frothy liquid seeping out of the can. Now I knew they liked me!

Especially when I was greeted with the cry, "Hey Willis. I didn't know they piled shit that high!"

Nor was I the only one to suffer at their hands. My old mate Derek Underwood, a great bowler but one of nature's camels when it came to enthusiasm on the field, was plodding manfully around the boundary in vain pursuit of the ball when someone in Bay 13 informed him, "Underwood—you're so bloody slow you've read all the adverts!"

Mind you, we Poms could get our own back if we waited long enough. That great umpire Dickie Bird set up Dennis Lillee and Rod Marsh beautifully one day during a tense period in an Ashes Test in England. Lillee was bowling wonderfully as only he could, and the English batsman was not really good enough to lay bat on ball. Four times in one over he was beaten all ends up by Lillee, who with Marsh, appealed for a caught behind, lbw—almost everything but handled ball. A Lillee/Marsh appeal never lacked conviction and they could hardly believe that Dickie Bird remained unimpressed. At the end of the over, Lillee glared at the umpire as he refused his sweater and the Yorkshireman snapped back, "I tell you what, Dennis, you two boogers will never die of curiosity!"

Another Yorkshireman—Geoffrey Boycott—could never share a joke about himself in the same way as the lovable Dickie Bird. To Geoffrey, cricket was an obsession, a way of justifying himself to a hostile world. A great batsman, but a selfish one. As a result, his reputation of running out his teammates was legendary. He was one of the great 'counters' I have seen. If the bowling was undemanding, you could bet your life that our Geoffrey would be looking to get a single near the end of the over to keep the strike.

Well one day he met his match. Geoffrey went out to bat with a rather tired old horse. After Geoffrey had given the horse the usual stuff about running when the master batsman said so, the horse took the first strike. 'Dobbin' proceeded to smash 24 off the first over, with a succession of brilliant strokes.

Geoffrey remained unimpressed and breathed a sigh of relief that at last he would take the second over. Off the first five balls, he played the classic copybook forward defensive stroke then, predictably, went for the quick single to pinch the strike. This time the horse refused to move from the crease and Geoffrey was run out by half the length of the pitch. "Why didn't ya roon?" he bellowed at the horse as he passed him. 'Dobbin' was quick to defend himself: "If I was that bloody quick, I'd be running at Flemington this afternoon, not standing here watching you make a prat of yourself!"

Pat Pocock, on the other hand, could take a joke about himself. Pat was a fine offspinner for Surrey and England for 20 years, but I remember him most for his passionate enthusiasm for the game. He never stopped talking about it—I swear he chatted cricket in his sleep—but one day he lost his famed sense of humour and became deadly serious. This was the day Pat decided to improve his undistinguished batting by wearing spectacles.

Some of us had thought for years that a new technique might have improved the Pocock batting average, but glasses seemed a step in the right direction. He went out to bat against Middlesex, feeling rather self-conscious about wearing specs for the first time. He knew he was due for a prolonged bout of leg-pulling and Pat was determined not to rise to the bait.

130

Fred Titmus prepared to bowl and, being a little deaf, had not heard the titters at the other end. Just as he was about to bowl, he noticed Pocock's glasses and shouted, "What the bloody hell are those?" Pocock responded with some severity, "A bloody hearing aid, what do you think?" Titmus proceeded to scatter his stumps with the first delivery, a perfect inswinging yorker that castled Pocock before he could get his bat down. Behind the stumps, John Murray, that great practical joker, said, "I reckon you need a hearing aid as well. You never heard that, let alone saw it!"

Happy days, great memories. I wish I could have shown my enjoyment of those times more openly when I was a player but I preferred the deadpan observations from the corner of the mouth, rather than the guffawing gusto of a Botham. However, I assure you I never lost sight of the fun to be had from the game and, as any retired cricketer will tell you, that stays in the memory longer than mighty deeds. Long may it continue.

by
Ian
Chappell

WAUGH GAMES

IN many of the Australia v West Indies matches during the 1988–89 season there were a number of strange umpiring decisions, many where the batsmen had quite obviously edged the ball to the wicketkeeper, but, for some reason, were given not out.

Some of the West Indies players were reminded of a similar style of umpiring in the Caribbean when they played under umpire Greg Waugh from the island of Dominion. He was standing in a game where offspinner Lance Gibbs found the edge and the 'keeper had gleefully accepted the catch.

Gibbs was enthusiastic in his appeal, but incredulous when umpire Waugh turned it down. "Why not out?" questioned Gibbs. "Because he only barely touched it," replied umpire Waugh.

SILENT NUMBER

BARBADOS is my favourite island in the Caribbean. It has an almost perfect climate and the locals are pretty relaxed. They have a saying 'soon come', which means anytime in the next couple of days.

I doubt they have any ulcer specialists practising on Barbados. If there are then they'd get no business from the room stewards at Kensington Oval. It was another perfect day as I sat on the players' verandah at Kensington in 1973.

Despite being at peace with the world I was in a state of hyperactivity compared with the four elderly room stewards. They were sitting back, eyes closed, heads against the pavilion wall, enjoying the warming sunshine. The wall telephone rang.

All four gentlemen continued to rest, eyes closed. Not a muscle twitched. No chance of a statue of Alexander Graham Bell being built on Barbados, I mused. Four rings, five rings . . . I was considering answering the infernal thing myself when the bloke nearest the phone opened an eye. Then he closed it again and went back to rest. Eight rings, nine rings . . . then finally it got to him.

Without opening his eyes he reached out his left arm and located the receiver on the wall. Lifting it out of its cradle he placed it against his ear. Still with his eyes closed he listened for about a minute without saying a word, then nodded and hung up.

LINE OF DEMARKATION
'BOO' Medford was one of the groundsman's assistants at Kensington Oval, Barbados, on my two tours to

the Caribbean. His actual title was 'line marker'; he painted the crease at both ends of the pitch. Before play, and at each break, 'Boo' would dutifully stand back with arms folded while the rest of the staff made the pitch ready for play. That done, 'Boo' would step forward with his paint pot and brush, and, with the concentration of Michelangelo he'd draw the white lines of the bowling and popping creases at both ends.

After play he could be prevailed upon to leave his groundsman's quarters by the promise of a cold Banks beer in the Australian dressing room. There 'Boo' would confide how much he liked the Australian way of playing the game.

One day of a Supertest in 1979, rain interrupted play with Australia batting and in a strong position. So I was keen to see the pitch covered quickly. When I saw the covers being taken out by wheelbarrow I suspected the ground staff didn't need to cover the pitch too often in Barbados.

When they unravelled the tarpaulins the wind blew them to all corners of the ground. I was getting angry: was this a Caribbean plot to liven up the wicket for the West Indies pace attack?

Then I saw 'Boo' strolling confidently to the middle. I relaxed. 'Boo's' years of on-the-job training would see to it that the young fellas got it right.

To my astonishment when 'Boo' got to the middle he just folded his arms and stood there watching. Eventually, some 20 minutes after commencing Operation Coverup, all the tarpaulins were gathered in and battened down on the pitch. I was livid.

When 'Boo' duly arrived at our dressing room after play had thankfully been called off for the day, I sailed into him. "For chrissakes 'Boo'," I remonstrated, "I thought you were on our side. Why didn't you help the young guys put the covers down?"

"Not my job," said 'Boo'. "I'm de line marker!"

by
Sunil
Gavaskar

SUNNY SIDE UP

MOST contests between two teams, or two individuals, begin with that ritual called 'the toss'. There are many ways to toss. Tennis and squash players spin the racquet and guess 'rough' or 'smooth'. Cricketers toss a coin and it can often decide the result of the match. I have known captains to get into a sweat about the toss. Why, even during the time I was captaining India I would spend sleepless nights tossing this way and that. In bed!

Seriously, the lesson of the toss is never to give your opponent any sympathy. No quarter. The Aussies say: "never give a sucker an even break." The toss is a learning process which never stops. That explains why some cricketers are called students of the game, but nobody is referred to as The Master. Mind you some have tried for that ultimate accolade.

Ashok Mankad, reckoned by many in India to be one of the canniest brains not to have led his country, was my captain at the college, university and first class levels. He was the one who drilled into us the importance of the toss with this story:

"In one of those needly club games my opposing skipper was a person who stammered. When I flipped the coin up in the air my adversary said 'hea . . . hea

136

"SORRY, FELLAS — WE LOST THE TOSS AGAIN!"

. . . hea . . .' but before he could get all of the word out, the coin had fallen. Heads were up. "So I quickly picked up the coin and told him that since his call had not been completed I would generously flick it again. This time I also tossed the coin a little higher. 'Hea . . . hea . . . hea . . . hea . . . hea . . .' I heard, but again the coin was too soon on the ground. As heads were again up, I turned to my opposing skipper, and, with a shrug of my shoulders and a smile, I tossed again. Higher.

"My adversary again trusted in 'hea . . . hea . . . hea . . .' but this time the coin fell 'tails'. I was triumphant. 'Hea . . . hea . . . heh, heh,' I said but the toss is 'tails'. You lose, we bat."

My first series as captain of India was at home against the West Indies in 1978. Their skipper was likeable, little Alvin Kallicharran. Big Clive Lloyd and other big guns were playing with white balls under the World Series lights. 'Kalli' was a half inch shorter than me so when we went out to toss I could put an arm around his shoulder without getting a cramp in mine.

Wickets in India start to spin appreciably towards the end of the match, sometimes even in the beginning! So to win the toss is to win the match. Ashok's lesson: a good captain never leaves to luck something as chancy as the toss. With that in mind I tossed with one coin for the whole series. It was a regular 50 paisa coin.

The only variable was that I ensured the side of the coin to be called heads would alternate each Test. By the Fourth Test 'Kalli' was suffering toss fatigue. Out we went, up went the coin . . . I groaned, for I had badly wanted to win this toss. But 'Kalli' had his hand outstretched and was congratulating me on winning the toss. The continual switching of heads had confused me! I think.

Many summers later at the same Delhi venue a toss win was again vital to India. The pitch looked exactly like the one way back in 1969–70 that had prompted Australia's Bill Lawry to predict he would go fishing on the fourth day. Where Bill was going to fish in Delhi remains one of the game's best secrets.

But the idea was right. When asked what I thought of the pitch I told the England supporters from Fleet Street if they had not seen the Taj Mahal they should plan to go there on the fourth day. England's batsmen had floundered against the legspin of Siva in the previous Test, and, now, to have Siva bowl against them in the fourth innings of this Test I needed to win the toss.

I walked out with the England captain, David Gower, who like 'Kalli' was an extremely nice guy. He came from one of those upper class British families. In all my years of playing against him I can't recall a foul word passing his lips. This was uppermost in my mind as we walked to the centre. I showed him the coin and showed him which side was 'heads'. But when I came to the 'tails' part I inquired as to why the flip side was still a 'tail' when the rest of the world was calling it an 'arse'.

I issued a gentle hint that he could start a new trend by calling 'arses' instead of 'tails'. David, God bless him, gave me one of his very warm, crooked smiles as he gently shook his head. Further prodding on my part brought laughter, and not even an assurance that there were no hidden pitch microphones could convince him he was free to call 'arses'.

For mine, I was convinced there was no way known David was going to call 'tails' when the coin went up. So a deft change of side-up as I placed the coin on my thumb increased the chances of it falling 'tails'. Sure enough David called 'heads' and the coin fell 'tails'.

As he bent to pick up the coin David had the rueful look of a man who thought he'd been had; as he beamed the winner's grin at the end of the Test I considered another lesson in the way of the toss: beware the captain who's been headed, he may give you the bum's rush!

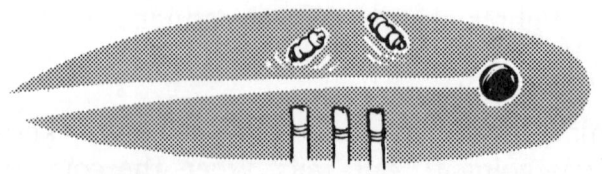

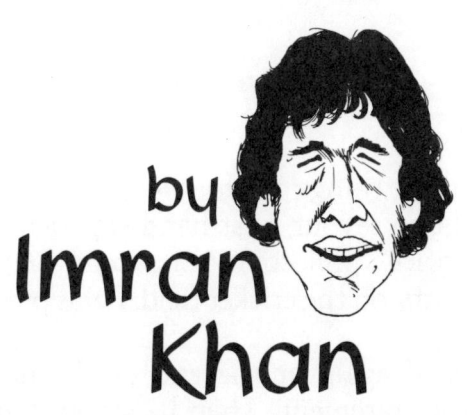

by
Imran
Khan

A MATTER OF WIFE AND DEATH

I played a lot of cricket with Sarfraz Nawaz and knew him as a pace bowler who always gave his all for his country. And I had never seen him as tense as he was during the final Test against the West Indies in Pakistan in 1980. So tense was he that he seemed to be in a world of his own.

I put his mood down to the delicate state of the series. We were one down (and on the way to losing our first home series since 1969) but had the tourists 6/120 and there was plenty of drama in the air. I was in the middle of a good spell and Sarfraz was bowling extremely well from the other end. We would pass at the end of each over and although there wasn't a lot of time for conversation, I'd walk across to him and say something like, "Come on—we can do it!"

The expression on his face was somewhat blank, yet deeply concerned. It was as if he was not hearing a word I said. He appeared to be staring into the distance. Ah, I thought, this is the ultimate expression of concentration and dedication. This is a man absolutely devoted to victory for his country.

I persevered with my "Come on—we can do it" routine and eventually Sarfraz replied. He looked directly and very intensely at me and said: "It is a matter

141

of life and death!"

Was this taking things too far? No, it was not. This was a moment to savour, first-hand experience of the "ultimate sacrifice" philosophy of a man prepared to die for his country on the cricket field. I was profoundly impressed.

As we crossed again at the end of the next over, he repeated the statement. Then he stopped and said: "You know, it is a matter of life and death because he says he's going to kill her!"

I had no idea what he was talking about. Certainly, I could not equate it with a game of cricket against the West Indies.

I learned later that Sarfraz had become romantically involved with a lady who happened to be married.

So much for dying for one's country on the field of cricketing endeavour!

HOT TOPIC

I couldn't help overhear a conversation between Javed Miandad and an English woman at a very formal cocktail party at the Pakistan Embassy in London during the 1987 tour. And just as I was about to rescue him from language difficulties, he confounded us all.

The lady was asking Javed polite questions about our country. "Does the Equator pass through Pakistan?" she inquired. "Pardon?" said Javed.

"Does the Equator pass through Pakistan?" Again, "Pardon?" I was about to step in and answer the lady's question, but a suddenly-inspired Javed beat me to it.

"Oh yes," he said knowingly, "Quetta is in Pakistan!"

MAGNANIMOUS MOSHIN

THE inverted logic of Moshin Khan made me smile the day he made his match-winning double century for Pakistan against England at Lord's in 1982. Moshin in fact made all those runs with a "foreign" bat.

Moshin had signed a contract with a certain bat manufacturer but was actually using a rival company's product. Don't ask me why. Sikander Bakht was playing with the bats Moshin was supposed to be using and told him the manufacturer wanted to know what was going on. "Why aren't you using their bats?" he asked. "You're taking money from the bat company."

"Well, yes," Moshin replied. "It's true I have taken money from them, but there's no problem. I'm playing with the other bats and have decided not to take money from that company."

by
Dennis
Lillee

HARD HATS AND HARD LUCK

FAST bowlers regarded the advent of the batsman's protective helmet as a step in the wimp direction. No-one likes to break heads, but we figured the short-pitched ball which whistled around the batsman's ear was a perfectly legitimate act of intimidation, an approved and very necessary weapon in our armoury.

I suppose that attitude lasted until the pacemen themselves took their next turn at the crease and faced a couple of thunderbolts. Suddenly that new-fangled headgear made a bit of sense.

Bruce 'Roo' Yardley was not a fast bowler. He was an offspinner who gave great service to Western Australia and Australia, and a better-than-useful down-the-order batsman who faced his quota of bouncers. He decided very early in the piece that helmets were an excellent innovation.

More than that, he went to the trouble of doing his own research, and came up with the very latest in headgear, a masterpiece called Protec. When he walked our wearing it people thought Neil Armstrong had overshot the moon.

Bruce gave his Protec its first airing in a Sheffield Shield match at the Sydney Cricket Ground, when W.A. were getting a hiding. Geoff Lawson and Lenny

Pascoe were bowling like the wind, 'smoke' coming out of their ears.

Lenny did a double take as 'Roo' walked on to the field in his far-out helmet. He followed Bruce all the way to the wicket, saying nothing, just looking.

Lawson was rearing to go, shifting impatiently from foot to foot at the start of his long run. "Hey, 'Henry'!" Pascoe yelled. "We've got a new helmet. Let's test it out for the manufacturer!"

Henry got the message; so did Bruce. Lawson's third ball took the off stump out of the ground—remarkably, the result of a full-blooded square cut played right off the meat of the bat.

Bruce's downfall was that he played the stroke while standing almost a metre outside leg stump! To me, that showed a lack of real faith in his shiny new Protec.

Having acquired his revolutionary hardhat, however, Bruce was not about to abandon it without exhaustive trial. He was wearing it again later that season against South Australia at the Adelaide Oval and he was going very well indeed.

As another of a series of square cuts off Wayne Prior scorched away to the boundary, the radio commentator was moved to remark that "Yardley's in full cry" and a spectator shouted "Great shot!"

"Yeah," muttered S.A. captain Ian Chappell, "It's the only bloody shot he's got."

At that point, Chappell took Ashley Mallett away from gully and dropped him two-thirds of the way back to the fence, but on the same line. It left open the way from cover to third slip for Bruce's favourite stroke. Chappell also instructed Prior to bowl the next ball right on the spot for the Yardley cut.

'Roo' took note of the field adjustment, reassured

himself that he was on a roll and that there was more room in the air than on the ground. Therefore, the huge gap Chappell had left was fair game. He would take South Australia on.

Prior bowled the next ball to instruction and Yardley put it straight down Mallett's throat. 'Roo' was cursing his stupidity as he began the long walk back to the pavilion, unbuckling his Protec as he went. Chappell was walking beside him.

"I wouldn't take that helmet off," Chappell said. "Your brains might spill!"

RETURNING THE FIRE

THERE are a couple of ways players can handle crowd violence in India. My preferred option, at the first suggestion of mob displeasure, was to run and hide. Switzerland rather appealed to me as safe ground. I learned at Hyderabad in 1979 that Rodney Hogg had a different approach.

Even when they're reasonably happy with the state of play, Indian spectators like to throw things when touring teams are in the field ... stones, bottles, anything they can lay their hands on ... and Rodney was copping plenty during a bowling spell this day. Hoggie bowled off a long run and a short fuse.

He disliked batsmen as much as any quick I have seen and his tolerance threshold towards idiots in the crowd was also quite low. It surprised us all on this occasion to see him pick up the assorted projectiles which came his way and stack them neatly beside his bowling mark.

Had he mellowed? Was he going to turn the other cheek? Rodney walked back to his mark for the last ball of his spell, looked at his pile of missiles, looked at the crowd—and pelted them with every piece of debris they'd thrown at him. The crowd rioted, of course.

West Indian fast bowler Sylvester Clarke ran into a similar situation while fielding on the boundary during a game in India. He was learning to live with the small stones raining in from the other side of the high wire fence (a standard fixture at all Indian grounds), but when half a house brick missed him by a whisker, he decided enough was plenty.

Sylvester picked up the brick and threw it back into the crowd, hitting a spectator and damn near killing him. There were lots of problems over the incident, but just how much is a player expected to take from these cretins?

I met Sylvester for the first time in Australia a few years later. He flashed one of those famous West Indian smiles and said: "Me Brickie!" And before I'd had time to respond: "And you Kickie!" He was referring, of course, to the contact between my boot and Javed Miandad's backside in a Perth Test.

I decided there and then that I liked Sylvester Clarke's style.

by
Alan
Knott

TOO MANY BEG PARDONS

THREE years into retirement now and one of the aspects of the life of a cricketer which I miss, and probably always shall, is the good humour—even when the laugh has been at my expense.

That's how it was at Old Trafford in 1981, during the Fifth Test against Australia. I had just caught Martin Kent off John Emburey and was standing chatting to my colleagues. Dennis Lillee emerged from the pavilion to walk to the crease, against the background noise of a ground announcement.

It wasn't very clear to me but everyone started clapping, on and off the field. I queried the applause with Ian Botham, who explained, straightfaced, "They announced something about a new record Dennis has achieved."

Naturally I started clapping, which prompted a man in the crowd to shout: "Stop showing off Knott." The England players broke up as Botham explained "The announcement was that you've just broken the record for a wicket-keeper's dismissals against Australia."

All my career there seemed to be incidents and announcements which I missed. I thought all the Kent players were having me on at Edgbaston during a Sunday League game against Warwickshire.

A dog wandered on to the pitch and held up play. That I noticed, but I certainly didn't see the dog cock its leg and give one of the stumps a drenching.

The Kent players were adamant it happened and it wasn't until I saw the highlights of the game on television that I realised it wasn't a joke. And that when I was busily taking my stance I was standing in it!

At Lord's, in another game for Kent, this time against Middlesex, there was a tough encounter with their West Indies pace bowler, Wayne Daniel, who was in his Benefit Year.

When I went into bat Wayne was bowling very fast and very aggressively, having already picked up a few wickets. The first two balls he bowled to me were both very quick bouncers—adequate proof to me that he was in a really fiery spell.

During the next over from Norman Cowans I stood at the non-striker's end, trying to fire myself up for my next encounter with Wayne. He was bowling so fast that I knew I had to be fully alert or I could get hit. Norman was walking back to his mark when, out of the corner of my eye, I saw Wayne moving towards me from mid-on!

Thinking I might be in for some verbal abuse I pretended not to see him. But he called out: "Knotty can you play in a benefit match for me at the end of the season?"

The conversation was halted because Norman was waiting to bowl his next delivery. When he was walking back to his mark again I called out to Wayne: "I'll have to check my diary for September."

The next over, he pounded in, even more hostile, and this time I had to contend with three bouncers, which whistled over my head. As he passed me at the end of the over I quickly said, "I'd love to play in September Wayne." He only gave me two bouncers in the next over!

A previous encounter with Wayne had not been so amusing from my point of view—I sustained a broken finger batting against him at Canterbury.

It was in 1976 when he was playing for the West Indies against Kent. The damage was done before tea and I went out to bat again after the interval.

Soon I realised it was much more serious than I had thought so I tried to get out. The move worked as I skied a ball from Albert Padmore high into the air and was caught, only to find the umpire had called no ball.

There was nothing for it but to retire hurt; the next morning I discovered the Press had reported I went off after being struck a painful blow on the finger by Padmore, the tourists offspinner!

Every batsman, of course, finds himself on the wrong end of a run-out incident but during the winter of 1973-74 it was a case of lightning definitely striking twice—and in quick succession.

My batting form was very disappointing and I joined Dennis Amiss, during the course of his magnificent innings at Sabina Park, Jamaica, when he made an unbeaten 262 which enabled England to draw the second Test.

Dennis played the ball to Clive Lloyd, called 'yes' and ran. Clive, then still the greatest cover fielder in the world, scored a direct hit on the stumps and that was the end of my innings.

Next we went on to play the Leeward Islands in Antigua and Dennis gave a repeat performance in our second innings. I had been promoted to number three to try and get out of my poor batting run and this time Dennis challenged a youngster called Viv Richards, at cover point. We were not to know then that he was to become one of the top fielders in that position.

As Dennis and I crossed in the middle of the pitch I called out, "Oh no, not again Den" and was run out by yards as Viv scored a direct hit on the stumps.

Then batting at Adelaide in a World Series Cricket game against the West Indies I was wearing a helmet for the first time. With the visor pulled down I hardly saw the first delivery and because of the helmet's sides I didn't hear Tony Greig's call for a single, either, when he turned the ball on the leg side.

Run out by half the length of the pitch, I returned to the pavilion to be asked by the interviewer on the outfield, former Australian Test cricketer, David Colley, about my dismissal. When he queried whether I had heard the call I could only reply, "Pardon?"

by
Merv
Hughes

BALL-TERROR

A pretty smart bloke once said, "cricket's a great leveller". One thing's for sure he wasn't sitting in Bay 13 at the time. My mates in that particular plot of eccentric cricket territory would have been more likely to come up with something more succinct, like, "one day the rooster, next day the feather duster". More colourfully expressed though, of course. Cricket is a bit like that. In the 1988–89 summer I played in four Tests, all against the West Indies, got 14 wickets and got tagged a hero—by my fellow Vics anyway! The summer before in the four Tests that I played I took 14 wickets, too— then got the sack! Yet last summer I got onto the Ashes tour to England.

"Doesn't matter", as Con the Fruiterer, King of Moomba would say. I enjoyed the season against the West Indies, and for sure my sweetest memories of cricket come from that summer. I particularly liked it when we won in Sydney. Of course I didn't play any part in the win at all. I did tell A.B. (Allan Border) I'd bowl some spin but you fair dinkum couldn't get the ball out of his hand!

Mind you, it was pretty hard to get the ball out of mine in the Second Test in Perth when 'Henry' Lawson copped that jaw-breaker. That was the match in which I managed one of the game's most unusual hat-tricks.

The truth is I didn't even know I'd taken it. I certainly knew I'd taken two wickets with successive balls, Patrick Patterson with the last ball of the West Indies first innings, and then Gordon Greenidge with the first ball of the second innings. But when Richie Richardson survived the next I was sure I'd done my dash. About two overs later Steve Waugh sidled up to me and said, "I think you might have taken a hat-trick."

"What do you mean?" I asked. "Well, in the first innings I think you got Curtly Ambrose with the last ball of an over, Patrick Patterson with the first of the next, then Greenidge with the first ball in the second innings."

Now, Steve's nickname in the team is 'Tugga', as in tug-o-war. And I reckoned there was a fair chance he was having a lend of me. "Are you sure?" I queried, and gave him a bit of the narrowed eyes treatment, and a bristle of the moustache, to go with my close-cropped hairstyle. "Yeah, pretty sure," he said. "I just heard it over the PA system."

You'll appreciate my nervousness about messages from team-mates when I tell you about waiting to go into bat in that same Test, which just happened to be my Comeback Test. I don't mind admitting that I've never been the most courageous of batsmen, and, watching the West Indies quicks firing them in on that cracking Perth pitch isn't my idea of entertainment. There I was, next in, sitting on the bench between David Boon and A.B.

Each had a brand new six-stitcher, and was tossing it from one hand to the other. Each time the ball made a sort of 'thwacking' sound, hard leather against flesh.

There'd be a 'thwack' and Boonie would say, "it sure doesn't tickle when you get hit with one of these!"

Then there'd be another 'thwack' and A.B. would say, "Jeez, that Ambrose is working up some pace!" Boonie: "second new ball's due, wonder if they'll take it?"

"Wonder?" I thought as I watched Tim May and 'Henry' Lawson emulating a couple of Diggers in the trenches at Gallipoli. "Wonder when, not if!"

The new ball was taken. I was, as they say in Bay 13, packin' it! Then poor Geoff Lawson copped that one on the jaw. 'Thwack', and I was in. I waited while they stretchered 'Henry' off. Then A.B. spoke. "We'll declare," he said. I could've kissed him!

The game was fun again, especially as we were to soon go into the World Series Cup limited overs games. The crowd noise at these games is astonishing. There's this constant murmur, and chanting, and they blow hooters and they do 'the wave'. It was at one of these

games, at the M.C.G., where the crowd, naturally in Bay 13, began mimicking my bowling warm-up aerobic sessions. All I could hear at first was a roar behind me, but when I turned the crowd was just its usual vocal, shifting self.

I said to Dean Jones between overs, "what the . . .'s going on with the crowd, mate?" He laughed, "they're mimicking your every move mate, why don't you try putting your foot in your mouth?" Later in the summer I joined Deano at the batting crease in the fifth Test in Adelaide. He was 173 not out. I was the second last batsman, with Mike Whitney to follow. Could we last long enough to help Deano get his double hundred?

I'd only been batting a little while before it seemed all of me was hurting, fingers, ribs, left arm, a shoulder, a foot, even my helmet was ringing. "Isn't it amazing," I thought, "how the ball aways seems to miss my chest pad." Dean had obviously noted my discomfort because he came down the pitch to give me some words of encouragement. He said, "Don't worry about your score, worry about my score." That seemed reasonable seeing as I was still a duck. I decided to attack the bowling. Next time I looked at the scoreboard I'd advanced to 45 and Deano was 193. My first Test match 50 was clearly in sight. I hurried down the pitch to Deano and said, "Don't worry about your score, worry about mine."

"Deano made 216 and I got 72 'red inks', the first time I can recall leaving the field with my bat raised. And when I got back to the rooms there were all my team-mates formed in a congratulatory semi-circle. A.B. was the first to speak: "Merv you could be Australia's leading allrounder—if you could get some wickets."

by Clive Lloyd

CHARLIE, IT'S FOR YOU

THE 1963 West Indies tour of England was just a little before my time (and it may surprise a lot of cricket fans to learn that *anything* was before my time). I wish I'd been on the scene because it was quite a series, that one, laced with outstanding individual performances, milestones and records. The cricket historians were kept very busy documenting achievements.

For example, the series opener gave the West Indies its first Test victory at Old Trafford. On top of our 5-0 defeat of India in 1961–62, it also gave us six consecutive Test wins for the first time. Opener Conrad Hunte's 182 in our first innings was the highest score against England at Manchester and Lance Gibbs' match analysis of 11/157 was his best in a career spanning 79 Tests.

You see what I mean about milestones. Oh, and for the trivia buffs, Surrey's Mickey Stewart, John Edrich and Ken Barrington became the first three players from one county to occupy the first three places in an England batting order. It is worth recalling, too, that this was one of the rare occasions at any level of cricket where a team required just one run in its second innings to win a match. I'm happy to say the target was achieved without loss, the single coming, very appropriately, from Hunte's bat.

The Second Test at Lord's was one of the most dramatic of cricket matches. When Wesley hall bowled the last ball, England had one wicket standing and needed six runs to win. Allen played the ball defensively to make it a draw.

Colin Cowdrey had returned to the crease after having his arm broken and was prepared to bat one-handed had he been called upon to face the bowling.

There was no such thing as Man-of-the-Match award in those days. Had there been, it would certainly have gone to Freddie Trueman for his match figures 11/152. And Trueman, that great Yorkshire fast bowler and character, wasn't finished with us yet. Not by a long way.

He came out in the Third Test, at Edgbaston, and levelled the series virtually with his own arm. Freddie took 5/75 in our first innings and 7/44 in our second, sweeping England to a 217-run win. He took his last six wickets in a 24-ball spell which conceded just one scoring shot, a four to Gibbs.

Trueman's performance did more than simply win a Test match. It sent a buzz around an entire country. It electrified England and set the stage for the "showdown of showdowns" in the Fourth Test.

On the face of it, the euphoria of every cricket-loving Englishman could be justified. If Trueman could take 23 wickets in two "away" games, what would he do on his beloved home turf at Headingley? And if his Yorkshire team-mate Phil Sharpe could top-score with an unbeaten 85 in his Test debut at Edgbaston surely he would make a century—perhaps a double century—before his adoring home crowd. Yes, the signs were very, very good.

Sad (for England) to say that Charlie Griffith, that frontline accomplice of Wes Hall, destroyed the dream. Charlie short-circuited England's pursuit of our very respectable first innings' 397 by returning the best figures of his career—6/36 from 21.5 fiery overs. England were all out for 174 and the euphoria was in tatters.

As opening bowlers for both Barbados and the West Indies, Charlie and Wes were great friends. And they were rooming together during that Headingley Test. The morning after Charlie's match-winning blitz, Wes was opening the mail and stopped at a letter addressed to: "West Indian opening bowlers, C/-Headingley Cricket Ground". He removed the contents, a single sheet of paper carrying the message: "Why don't you go back home, you big ugly, black baboon!"

"Hey Charlie, there's a letter for you," said Wes.

YOU KNOW IT, YOU FIND IT!

A lot of people (non-West Indians, of course) are inclined to interpret the Vivian Richards swagger as a show of arrogance. I think it is an unfair assumption because Viv had the swagger long before he became widely regarded as the best batsman in the world. I rather think he was born with it. He has never lacked self-confidence—indeed he is very much a confidence player—but no, the "Richards strut", if you like to call it that, is merely a characteristic, a part of the man himself.

The impression that it may be an expression of arrogance has brought him into verbal exchanges from time to time with opponents, and he handles himself almost as well in these jousts as he handles a cricket bat. I recall with particular amusement his brush with a fiery young up-and-coming fast bowler during a West Indies tour of England in which I was captain.

The approaching confrontation between the local hero and master batsman Richards was billed as the highlight of this particular tour fixture—and neither player let the publicists down.

I won the toss, elected to bat and for a while things went very well for the quickie. He picked up a couple of wickets, which brought Viv swaggering to the crease, and his first delivery to him, predictably was a bouncer. Surprisingly, it caught Richards off guard and playing forward. A very good bouncer, it was, and a very near thing for Viv. He managed to weave out of its path but suffered the indignity of having his headgear spun back-to-front.

His second ball was also a beauty, Viv played forward to an outswinger which found the outside edge and flew between slips to the boundary.

It was the fast bowler's turn to strut now and he wasn't about to let two moral victories in successive balls against Richards go unacclaimed. "Look you, boyo," he shouted down the wicket, "Don't you know what the bloody ball looks like. It's red and round and it weighs five-and-a-half ounces!"

Viv said nothing. He twirled his bat, took another look around the field and awaited the next delivery. The third ball wasn't quite up to the standard of its forerunners. It was slightly overpitched and Viv launched himself and his massive bat at it. The ball soared over the long boundary, over a timberyard adjoining the ground and into a river adjoining that. It was a massive hit and the bowler's mouth was agape as he followed the ball's path out of the ground.

Viv strolled slowly down the wicket replacing imaginary divots with the tip of his bat. When he drew within earshot of the shattered bowler, he delivered the telling punchline. "Man," he said, "you know what it looks like—you bloody well go and find it!"

by
Jeff Thomson

DIAL 'M' FOR MURDER

SEVERAL Australian players took their wives along on the 1985 tour of England and I was lucky enough to have Cheryl and Matthew, our only child at the time, travelling with me. I loved having them along, but it must be said that an Ashes tour is something less than all beer and skittles with the added responsibility of having a wife and child in tow. There are problems, particularly in the areas of accommodation and the day-to-day necessities.

For example, given the opportunity, Cheryl and I would have dined out most nights, but young Matthew's needs and routine were paramount to us and that meant we ate in with him at the juvenile evening meal time around 6.30pm. Our first opportunity for dinner minus Matthew came on the second night of our stay at Chelmsford, where the Australians were playing Essex.

Graeme Wood, who was travelling with wife Angela and daughter Brook, told us the hotel provided a child-minding, or rather a child-listening service. He had taken advantage of it the previous evening. "All you do," he said, "is phone the front desk just before you leave, tell them you're going out and that you'll leave the phone off the hook. The staff at the desk then listen in for any disturbance in your room."

Because we were going to be no further away than the hotel restaurant anyway, it sounded quite satisfactory. I dutifully went down to reception while Cheryl was getting Matthew ready for bed and asked the girl how I went about arranging the service. I was told to return to our room, lift the phone and asked for the operator. This I did.

A woman answered the phone and I said: "May I have the operator, please?" She asked if I was Mr. Thomson and I said yes. A few seconds later the operator came on to the line. I explained I had been led to believe that he would monitor the phone in our room to make sure my baby was sleeping while I took my wife to dinner.

"I'm not going to do that," he replied. "Now hang on a minute!" I said. "I've just been downstairs, I spoke to the girl at reception and she told me to go back up to my room, ring the operator and all would be arranged. Now I'm going down to dinner and I want you to listen for my child while we are out of the room."

"No I'm not going to do that, mate," he said.

I was becoming very annoyed and I think I showed it. "Listen here, you dickhead," I said, "I've just spoken to Graeme Wood next door and you did the same thing for him last night. Why won't you do it for me?"

"I am not going to do anything of the sort and while we're at it, why don't you bloody go home, you Aussie bastard," he replied.

I was fast approaching boiling point on the Thomson scale. "Listen, you bloody Pommie idiot," I bellowed. "I'll come down there, pull your head off and stuff it somewhere very painful. I've had a gutful of this joint, a gutful of this country, the whole lot. Now what's your name because I'm going to take this further."

"Why don't you just pack it in and go home," he said.

"That's it. You're gone. You're dead!" I roared.

A very bewildered Cheryl had been listening to my side of the "conversation", wondering just what was going on. By now I was in a towering rage.

I slammed down the phone, stormed out the door and into the lift, just as Simon O'Donnell was getting out. He took one look at me and said, "What's the matter, Two-Up?" "I'm just going down to commit murder on the f . . . operator!" I said. "Oh," said Simon, "I'll go with you. I don't want to miss this."

When we reached reception, I yelled, "Who's in charge

here, because I want to get some answers. I've had enough of the rudeness and insults of your staff and I want an explanation!"

A young lady, mouth slightly agape, listened to my tirade and asked what she could do to help. "Just tell that rude, obnoxious operator to get himself out here," I said, "I'm going to fix him, I've had enough of that smart-arse."

"What do you mean?" she asked. "That bloke, the operator," I said "Get him out here. The idiot I was just arguing with!"

"But there's no male on duty tonight, sir," she told me.

At this stage I felt that I was being thwarted at every turn and I thought they were trying to protect the culprit from my rage and his just deserts.

"Now look," I said "let me get it right. I went upstairs to my room phone, asked for the operator and spoke to a bloke. Now where is he?"

"Oh", said the lady, "was that you?"

"Of course it was me! I was only doing what you'd told me to and I've had a run-in with this bloke and now I want to know where he is."

The lady blushed quite noticeably. "Oh dear," she said. "Was that you asking for the operator?"

"Yeah, that's right, just as I was told."

"I'm terribly sorry," she said. "but the operator to whom you were talking was not a member of our staff. I forgot all about our conversation and when you asked to be put through to the operator I switched you through to the international operator!"

Somewhere in England there is probably still a certain international telephone operator convinced that all Aussies are deranged.

by
Gordon
Greenidge

Two Bum Steers

CRICKET crowds the world over have their own particular brand of wit. In the West Indies it tends to be biting and, if you're not accustomed to it or take it too seriously, it can get you down at times. And it is directed at anyone the spectators feel merits it, Test star or first-timer.

Take Wayne Daniel, for instance. Wayne was one of the fastest bowlers we've had and a very good one, too. Perhaps if he had come along at a different time and not when there were so many contenders for the fast bowling spots around, he would have played more Test cricket for the West Indies. He had a great record for Middlesex and, whenever he came back home to play for Barbados in the Shell Shield competition, he usually did well.

But he would sometimes have off-days—don't we all!—and this was one of them. He just kept pitching up half-volley after half-volley and almost every one went crashing to the boundary with a big drive. The home crowd at Kensington Oval wasn't liking it very much and was vocal in its comments and advice.

As it happened, there had been a story in the papers that morning about the arrival of a big shipment of Mini-Mokes from Australia, the jeep-type vehicles that the tourists get around in when they're in Barbados. Amidst all the shouting from the stands came one clear voice that had us all falling about in the middle: "Hey, Daniel, you must have come in with that Mini-Moke shipment. Everybody's driving you!"

At the Queen's Park Oval Trinidad, there's a section of the crowd that sits in what's known as the Concrete Stand that has made the same reputation for itself as Bay 13 at the M.C.G. or the Hill at the S.C.G. Those who sit there don't miss a ball—or a trick. They are noisy and constantly make comments that get louder as the day goes on and the good Trinidad rum gets to work. One character, who delights in the nickname "Blue Food", has perfected the art of blowing a conch shell that echoes out like a fog horn every time the West Indies hit a boundary or get a wicket.

And, being Trinidadian, from the land of calypso and steel band, they love to sing. You never know what they might come up with next. At the end of the first Test of the 1978 Test against Australia, we all assembled in front of the Queen's Park pavilion for the presentation ceremony and the crowd, including the lot from the Concrete Stand, gathered around.

Bobby Simpson had been recalled to lead that Australian team which didn't include any of the players in Kerry Packer's World Series Cricket and it was badly beaten, by an innings, in three days as we *did* play our strongest team, W.S.C. players and all. Well, at least for the first two Tests.

True to form, the Concrete Stand started to sing but we were all baffled at first as they went into a song we all used to sing as kids. But they had a sharp twist to the end!

"Oh dear, what can they matter be,

"Oh, dear, what can they matter be,
"Oh, dear, what can they matter be
Simpson bring down a shit side!"
Even the Aussie boys cracked up and it was some time before we could get some order back to get on with the presentation!

HEAVEN'S ABOVE

WHEN you travel the world as much as we have to for international cricket these days you get used to a variety of accommodation. Some hotels can be palatial, others quite basic. You learn to take them very much as they come.

When we were in New Zealand following our tour of Australia in 1979–80, we came across some unusual accommodation, to say the least. We were usually in motels and the rooms were so small that it was almost impossible to cram in our gear and some of our big fast bowlers at the same time. But that was not Alvin Kallicharran's problem when we arrived at one venue quite late one evening.

When 'Kalli' got to his room, we heard him making a fuss. So we went across to see what it was all about. There was little 'Kalli', one of the smallest members of the team, looking up to a huge bed and looking puzzled. To get up to it, he had to climb a small ladder and 'Kalli', who had had a hard day in the field, quipped: "At least they could have installed a lift!"

168

by
Lance Cairns

One Highly-Strung Hippie

TIMES, obviously, have changed a great deal since I was first chosen in 1973 to represent New Zealand. The occasion was our first official cricket tour of Australia.

Sponsorship was unheard of in those days so it was up to the player to personally buy and pay for everything he was going to need on the trip—and that included his own bat. A detailed list arrived by mail from the New Zealand Cricket Council and, being a new boy, I thought it a must that I have everything on it. I was to learn later that some of the more senior members of our party were not quite so conscientious.

The requirements went all the way down to the dimensions of the suitcase and of the two strips—one black, one white—which must be painted on either side of it. I always wondered about the purpose of those painted strips; I assumed it was to make for easy identification at travel terminals.

Along with the itemised list came a written pep-talk reminding us that we were representing our country, were therefore ambassadors and our conduct on and off the field must be of the highest order.

Back in 1973, Jeremy Vernon Coney was a most unlikely ambassador. In time, he was to become a very fine ambassador and captain of his country. But in 1973

170

he looked like something out of a hippie commune.

Jerry was a student then, a most unkempt student with the regulation long, unwashed hair, the regulation ratbag clothing. He also had two of the smelliest feet in New Zealand. His Mother was very strict about him wearing socks, but because he had only the one pair, it was very difficult for him to wash them regularly and keep faith with Mum as well.

Coney was a late starter on that tour. He was summoned to cover for Glenn Turner, our incomparable opening batsman, who broke a finger while playing off the front foot in one of our early games.

Our student travelled light. His off-field gear consisted of the clothes he arrived in—and they weren't too flash, I can tell you. His cricket boots were at least five-years-old and had certainly never been cleaned. The sprigs were worn down to the soles, which were attached to the uppers by rolls of white (pardon, off-white) adhesive tape. He had one pair of batting gloves, the type with rubber spikes, and creams that nowhere near made the trip down to his ankles.

And his bat. . .ah, his bat. That was a masterpiece. Boldly emblazoned on the back in black, felt-tip print were the words 'Onslow Fourths', proud testimony that it had come all the way up through the ranks with its extraordinary owner. Great chunks of this piece of willow were held in place with white tape, off the same roll as that which saved his boots from disintegration. And the handle was broken.

Bob Vance, our tour manager, took one long look at the newly-arrived Jerry and decided that while individuality had its place, it was not wanted on this particular ambassadorial cricketing mission. Australia might not yet be ready for J.V. Coney.

Bob summoned Jerry to his hotel room and gave him quite a lecture on how important it was to look and act the part. Spruce up your act, my boy, or else! And having said that, he gave him $100—quite a lot of money at that time, and certainly more than Jerry had seen at any one time. It came with strict instructions to go downtown and buy himself some decent clothes and cricket gear. And a haircut. Definitely a haircut.

We were all very keen to see this new-look, cut-and-polished, scrubbed-up Jerry Coney, but when he returned from his shopping spree four hours later, nothing had changed. Still the long, untidy hair, the jeans, T-shirt and jandels (thongs). As scruffy and unambassadorial as ever.

But wait... there *was* something new! Yes, something had been added, a $100 twelve-string guitar.

THE CONGO LINE

I DIDN'T have to be told, when we left New Zealand for Australia on my maiden tour in 1973, that you didn't mess with the skipper. Bevan Congdon had a reputation as a tough taskmaster, a guy who thought nothing of holding up a game in the middle of an over to walk across from gully and blast a bowler for serving up a half-volley. I'm sure he would have put squarely in their place a few young upstarts who play the game today.

'Congo' was also known to be very fair, and there was nothing austerely aloof about him. He made a point, in fact, of rooming with the new guys on tour to make them feel more at ease and to get to know them better at a personal level.

I drew the straw to room with Bevan in Perth when we played Western Australia, and it was during one of those heatwaves over there when the "Fremantle Doctor" didn't arrive. The first three days were played in severe heat and we were warned that the fourth and last would be even worse.

Now I've always liked to enjoy myself and I particularly enjoyed the night out before we had to face that real scorcher. It's hard to remember now if the movies came out later than usual or if we found a good party. I suspect it was the latter because we got back to the hotel at 2.00am.

It was an unwritten rule in the sharing situation that first one to bed would leave the bathroom light on so the later arrival wouldn't disturb him—or injure himself—by falling over something in the dark on his way to the cot. That night, I opened the door to total darkness.

Hell, I thought, a bit of care needed here. Don't want

to wake the skipper and give myself away. A very furtive Lance Cairns undressed just inside the door, silently hung his clothes in the wardrobe and stole across the carpet into bed. Mission accomplished—and not a peep out of the skipper. I should have been a commando! Or at least a cat burglar.

'Congo' was his normal self in the morning. He asked quite casually what time I'd got in and I told him "about 11 or 12." Nothing more was said about it and I was on very good terms with myself when we arrived at the W.A.C.A. Ground.

The weather forecast was spot-on because it was already fiercely hot when Bevan threw me the ball to open the bowling. I was still bowling—and it was just that much hotter—when drinks arrived an hour later. And I was still bowling when lunch mercifully intervened.

I was still bowling 1½ hours after lunch, and if W.A. hadn't declared at that happy point I believe I would still have been trundling in at stumps.

As it was, I'd bowled 3½ hours unchanged in some of the most savage heat I've experienced.

The skipper didn't say a word, and neither did he have to. The message was quite clear, as clear as the moral of this story: if you're rooming with your captain, and your captain happens to be a guy like 'Congo' Congdon, don't break the curfew!

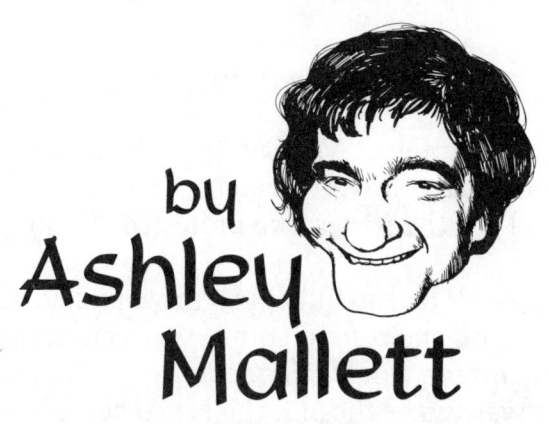

by Ashley Mallett

RAISING A RIOT

THE huge Indian police chief strode on the riot-torn ground in Bombay and suggested very seriously, "take one or two before you go." He was inviting this Australian team to go down fighting, to take a few rioters with us on our way to becoming just another set of statistics in the archives of Indian mob violence.

You could only blame the Victorians for putting all our lives at risk that November day in 1969. No-one else had appealed when Brian Taber, our wicketkeeper, accepted the ball which had beaten Venkat's bat by several inches. Taber tossed it to Keith Stackpole at second slip, but Stacky was in the air in a spontaneous appeal with bowler Allan Connolly, captain Bill Lawry at mid-on and Paul Sheahan at cover. Only Victorians would make such a frivolous appeal—yet incredibly, Venkat was given out, caught behind. Tourists get little charity from Indian umpires, so this was a total reversal of form.

Venkat was clearly miffed by the decision and didn't want to leave. When he saw he was going to get no sympathy from the Australians—and certainly no recall from Lawry—this little Indian off-spinner slunk away, head bowed, bat trailing. The crowd was unhappy.

So was the official scorer, who ran on to the ground

yelling for our captain: "Mr. Lorrie. . .Mr. Lorrie?" Bill asked him to please leave the arena, or words to that effect. "But I am the scorer," he protested. "I am going home."

Okay. Now we had an unhappy crowd and no scorer. Not to worry on the second count, we were told. The radio commentator would keep score.

And that was where the plot thickened because while the chorus of Victorian appeals may have set the scene for the riot, it was the radio man who actually incited it.

A lot of the fans there that day must have taken notice of national advertisement on page two of the local telephone book calling on all married males who had sired two or more children to have a vasectomy. The reward for having what a lot of women call the "kindest cut of all" was a free transistor radio.

Yes, there were many at Brabourne Stadium that day watching the cricket and listening to the commentary on their new trannies.

They would certainly have heard the commentator say, when Venkat was given out: "Lawry is a cheat. Venkat was not out. Lawry should recall Venkat. The man clearly was not out. He missed the ball by a very big margain. Lawry is a cheat."

And so the seeds of a riot were sown. And the simmering anger quickly erupted into full-scale violence. Bottles were thrown on to the field, chairs stacked high and set alight. Outside the ground, cars were overturned and burned. A nearby tennis club was torched.

We reached the relative safety of the dressingroom by running a gauntlet of deck chairs thrown by outraged members, barricaded the doors and very nervously drank a beer while the hostile crowd milled outside.

A very apprehensive Fred Bennett, our manager, brought us up to date on the situation. "Things are getting very dark out there," he said. "There are 10,000 very angry people out there all calling for Bill Lawry's blood!"

Fred was usually unflappable and had done a splendid job in India, a tour which is always difficult to manage. But as the late Les Truman, a former assistant manager, would have said: "Thank God for Dougie Walters."

Doug was famous for his timing—with bat and wit—and he was spot-on again in our seige situation.

He wiped the suggestion of a spot of beer froth from his upper lip and said: "They want Lawry, you say, Fred? Well, that's easy. Give the mob Lawry and let's get on with some serious drinking!"

You hear a lot about the decisions Indian and Pakistani umpires see fit to give, but you really have to be out there in the middle to fully understand how bad they can be. At best, at kindest, you would say the umps take patriotism to extraordinary lengths. And while their decisions may infuriate touring teams to the point of threatening to pack their bats and balls and go home, they inevitably give rise to light moments.

It wasn't long after the Brabourne Stadium riot that Australia was in trouble of a different kind on the 1969 tour. This time it was Bangalore and we were 8/65 in response to 359. Ray Jordan, partnering Bill 'The Rock' Lawry, faced the last ball before tea and was given out to a bat-pad catch at short leg.

"No bloody way did I hit that ball," Ray said at the time. I have no doubt he would say precisely the same thing if you were to ask him about it today.

He swore his innocence all the way in to the pavilion and was still swearing it towards the end of the tea adjournment. Some-one suggested he take his case all the way to the top—to the umpire who had sent him on his way.

That appealed to Ray's sense of fair play and he sought out the offender in the umpire's room just before play resumed. "There's no bloody way I hit that ball, umpy, no blo-o-ody way!" he said.

The umpire met Ray's angry glare, stood his ground and replied: "Ah, Mr. Jordan, now if you didn't hit that ball, I can tell you you were welly much LBW, Mr. Jordan. Welly much LBW."

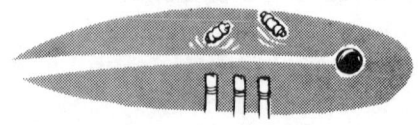

GETTING HIS EYE IN

THE name "Lord's Taverners" might imply a bunch of past cricketers who spend most of their waking hours at the Lord's Tavern reliving bygone glories over too many pints of English beer. To think that would be to do them a grave injustice. Don't think for a moment that they don't enjoy a pint, but there is much more to them than that.

The Taverners are, in fact, cricketers and actors who are dedicated to the game and to the less-fortunate who want to succeed in it.

Charity matches are their main fund-raisers and it was during one of these games that Colin Milburn was bowling to Ed Devereaux. Neither man really needs an introduction, but I'll play it safe and remind you that Milburn is the former powerhouse England batsman whose career was tragically cut short by a serious eye injury in 1969 and Devereaux the veteran Australian actor still probably best known for his role in 'Skippy the Bush Kangaroo.'

Devereaux nonchalantly leant on his bat that day and watched Milburn pick up his glass eye, which had fallen to the pitch as he followed through on his third delivery, and replace it in the socket.

The umpire was somewhat aghast. "Good God, Devereaux," he said, "did you see that?"

"Ah yes," Ed replied. "Milburn always takes three balls to get his eye in."

by
Derek Underwood

REDUCED TO ASHES

THE 1974-75 Ashes tour of Australia was the toughest in my experience as an England Test player. This was the 'Dennis Lillee/Jeff Thomson' tour—and didn't they blitz us! The battering we took couldn't help but affect our morale. Thankfully, we had a few real characters in that touring party—and an excellent manager, Alec Bedser—who did so much to hold us together.

To me, David Lloyd did more than anyone else to keep our spirits intact. He could always produce something to snap us out of our depression after another day's exposure to the ferocity of those terrible Aussie twins. David broke the silence in our dressing-room one evening by picking up a piece of paper and a pen and feigning a letter home. "Dear Mum," he said, "Am ducking and weaving well. I got a half-volley today —in the nets—and didn't know what to do with it."

David was a very good medicine for a shell-shocked and dejected team of English cricketers. Later in the season he took a painful blow in the groin from a Thomson delivery, which broke his protector. As he was assisted from the field, he stole a line attributed to the late Wally Grout and said: "Don't rub them —just count them!"

Yes, there was little to recommend that tour from

an England viewpoint, yet it provided me with one of my career highlights. In the First Test in Brisbane, I partnered Tony Greig in what I rate as the finest innings of his career. My role was strictly second fiddle, but it was great to be involved out there as Tony taunted

Lillee by using his height on a very lively pitch to drive him on the up. You could see Dennis's temperature rising as Tony stood there signalling four.

All very well for Greigy, I thought, but what about poor Derek Underwood at the other end? I saw a real danger of Dennis taking out his displeasure on a very much the lesser of the two batsmen.

Between overs I walked down the pitch to remind Tony that I was out there in the firing line too and not quite as capable of defending myself as he was. "Don't worry about Lillee," Tony assured me. "He's over the hill!" As if to prove the point which was to be disproved many times over that summer, he jumped up and pretended to head soccer-style, the next Lillee bouncer.

I'll never forget that innings. My contribution to a 58 run partnership was minor, but I lingered there against the full fury of a very fearsome attack for 90 minutes.

I allowed myself an inward grin when Dennis finished his spell and was replaced by Doug Walters. Now this was the sort of stuff I could handle, I thought. I was caught at cover off Doug's first delivery. Deceived by the non-pace—or that's what I've told myself ever since.

BOYCOTTED!

GEOFF Boycott, that dourest of opening batsmen, owes me something. He once deprived me of the honour of opening an innings for England. It was the only position in which I never batted for my country.

It was during the 1979-80 tour of Australia and we had 20 minutes to bat before stumps. I approached the skipper, Mike Brearly and volunteered my services as an opener for the sake of old England, of course. No thoughts of personal glory, I can assure you.

"Why risk Geoff?" I said. Mike agreed, but Geoff wouldn't hear of it. "I'm opening," he insisted. "It's my job. Nobody's having my place."

Several minutes later, Dennis Lillee sent down a magnificent ball and Geoff did very well to get a glove to it. Boycott, c Marsh, b Lillee. Another prized scalp for the old firm.

I'd put the pads on just in case, but hoping very deeply that I wouldn't be required. I couldn't resist it as I passed a very annoyed Geoff Boycott on my way to the crease: "A hard job, this nightwatchman business, isn't it?"

Geoff barely spoke to me for the rest of the tour and apparently he still hasn't forgiven me. He wrote of me in his book: "Derek has the appearance of a choirboy, the demeanour of a civil servant and the ruthlessness of a rat-catcher."

Does that make me a man of many parts?

by
John
Morrison

FROM THE PADDINGTON END

CRICKETERS traditionally return from a tour of India and/or Pakistan with hair-raising tales of sub-standard living, crook food, undrinkable water and shocking umpiring. Having made the trip to the sub-continent once, with New Zealand in 1976, I too can vouch for the whole catastrophe. But that's not the point of my story.

Our first game on that 1976 tour was in Peshawar, in far northern Pakistan, near the Khyber pass. It is a place where a lot of women get around with veils over the heads and, by the look of the few female faces we actually saw, it is probably just as well. I believe that during an M.C.C. tour a few years earlier, someone hit a six and a veiled woman took a brilliant catch in the crowd. So I suppose it's a question of who's watching who.

It being the tour opener, we were all very keen to do well at Peshawar. Accordingly, we were a little tense—and that *before* we got on the team bus for the ground. By the time we arrived there an hour late, we had learned the real meaning of traffic chaos, complete with donkey carts, camels and thousands of pedestrians who seemed to have a common death wish.

I think it would be reasonable to describe the trip

as a nightmare, and the dressingrooms which awaited us fitted in to the general scheme of things. Richard Collinge solved one problem—a veritable army of ants had taken over the room—by throwing a curried egg against a far wall. As the ants trooped off to enjoy their unexpected feed, they left us enough space in which to change into our gear.

Because we were so late, a lot of the pre-game rituals peculiar to cricket in India and Pakistan had to be dispensed with. Glenn Turner, our captain, was hustled out to toss the coin and returned with the news that I would be opening the batting with him. He was followed into the room by the umpires, who announced that "play would start in four minutes please."

Four minutes? FOUR MINUTES??? Yes please.

That took care of any thoughts of donning the pads at leisure and relaxing a while to get oneself into the state of mind which batsmen find conducive to successfully opening an innings. No, mild panic was called for here.

In my case, it was a little more than mild because my wife, Kathy, is superstitious. She had always had a thing about good-luck charms, which meant that I had to carry extra luggage to accommodate such essentials as every pair of socks in which I had made 17 not out (17 being her favourite number).

I rummaged frantically through my gear to find thigh pads, jockstrap etc. and was thrust out on to the field to meet the umpires' deadline and to face the music. Not until I was halfway to the wicket did I become aware of a large bulge in my trouser pocket.

It is not easy to examine a large bulge in your trouser pocket when you're walking out to open a game of international cricket without attracting unwanted attention, but by the time I reached the wicket I had identified my 'passenger'. It was a little pink teddy bear. Attached to it were a couple of nice little notes from my wife wishing me luck. She had obviously planted this quaint token of affection in the pocket as she packed my bags back home.

Lovely thought, dear, but what was I going to do with this furry little fellow as I took block in a tour opener in the depths of Pakistan?

I'll never forget the faraway look in the little Pakistani umpire's eyes when I asked if he'd mind holding my teddy while I batted.

Thank God it wasn't a Barbie doll!

'CRASH' FROM THE COAST

THAT I got to know Clive 'Crash' Albridge, is thanks to my involvement several years ago in the New Zealand Ambassador's side which toured South America, the West Indies, Europe, Britain, then back through Bermuda and the United States.

The team was a real assortment in terms of ability and origins and Clive was quite the most interesting character. He was a coal miner from Granity, on the West Coast of New Zealand's South Island. Cricket at Granity bore little resemblance to the norm.

Because his surname started with 'A', Clive was first on the tour roster to look after the baggage, which involved driving a truck from the airport to the hotel. That may sound a simple enough assignment, but when you've never really been adrift of Granity, a place like Buenos Aires must seem very big indeed. It was his driving in South America which earned him the nickname 'Crash' because he managed five separate skirmishes with things as diverse as other vehicles, power poles and ornamental gardens.

Mind you, one mustn't be too critical because the standard of driving among South Americans is appalling. It is the only place in the world where everyone stops at green lights because they know very well no-one's going to stop at the red ones.

Clive had no great claim to cricketing fame and was diplomatically left out of the early games of our tour. He had to be given a game eventually, though, and his big chance came when we moved on from South America to the West Indies. His debut was against Antigua, who batted first and declared at 4/350, which included a century from a fellow named Vivian Richards.

The NZ Ambassador's XI was looking particularly shaky at 5/31 in reply when Clive 'Crash' Albridge strode purposefully to the crease.

I was at the non-striker's end, which seemed like a good place to be because the ball was in the hand of one Andy Roberts, who had three wickets to his name and was bowling very, very fast. But reputations meant little to the coalminer from Granity, who stopped to assure me that he was no poofter, that they bred 'em tough on the West Coast, and, don't worry, he wouldn't let us down.

'Crash' took block with his Granity No 21 bat (Len Hutton autograph). His green-spike gloves, Jack Hobbs boots and David Livingston hat all bore the tacit expression of defiance.

The wicket-keeper and slips were standing 25 yards back as Roberts wheeled in. He bowled a rip-roaring bouncer which whistled perhaps a centimetre past Clive's ear and was still more than head high when it thudded into the 'keeper's gloves.

You had to admire Clive. Had he flinched? No sir. Had he moved a muscle at all? No way. Had he seen the ball at all? Certainly not.

A very pale and very shaken Clive Albridge walked down the wicket, clutched my arm and said: "Christ, John, there's nothing like this on the West Coast!"

by Jeff Dujon

LOVE IS A LONG INNINGS

GEOFF Boycott's always someone I've enjoyed chatting to about cricket. I don't know of anyone so wrapped up in the game and anyone who has studied batting as closely.

We were talking in the S.C.G. dressing room during the Fourth Test against Australia when Allan Border wrecked the West Indies. Naturally the conversation turned to batting on turning pitches when Keith Arthurton, one of the young players in the West Indies team, came up and listened intently. I could see he was fascinated by Geoff's theories.

After a while, he turned to Geoff and said: "You know, you must really like batting!"

"No, son," came the instant reply. "The good ones like it. The *great* ones *love* it".

FAST AND FURIOUS

KEEPING wicket for the West Indies for almost 10 years has been a thrill and an experience. Standing 25 yards back to the great fast bowlers the West Indies have had in that time sure beats taking guard against them in front of the stumps. It has given me a perfect vantage point to see how some of the top batsmen from other countries deal with them, and I tell you, I've learned a lot doing just that.

Just to put the record straight, West Indian batsmen have to face up to them back home in our Red Stripe Cup tournament as well and I've also been in the privileged position behind the stumps to see Gordon Greenidge and Desmond Haynes open the batting for Barbados against our Jamaica attack comprising Patrick Patterson, Michael Holding and Courtney Walsh. Privilege is not quite the word I would use for the feeling of meeting a Barbados quartet of Malcolm Marshall, Joel Garner, Wayne Daniel and Sylvester Clarke in the days when I was still fighting to make my way into the Test team! And, in those games, there's no quarter asked, and none given.

I have yet to come across a batsman who comes out to face that kind of pace without some trace of nerves. Some hide their feelings better than others but there's always a little tell-tale sign.

It wasn't difficult to recognise it in Ken Rutherford, the young New Zealander, during the final Test of their series in the West Indies in 1985. He was a very promising player on his first tour but he was like a lamb to the slaughter. Marshall was then bowling at his fastest and he was backed up by Joel Garner, Winston Davis and Courtney Walsh. If memory serves me right, poor Rutherford's scores going into the final Test were 0, 0, 4, 0, 2 and they dropped him down the list to No. 5 for that match. But, as fate would have it, he had come in on the second day just as Jeremy

"NOW, WHY ON EARTH WOULD THE BOWLER WANT THE SIGHT SCREEN MOVED?"

Coney walked off with a fractured forearm after taking a blow from Garner.

Rutherford was white as a sheet as he came in—and chewing away feverishly. First ball, he took a blow on the helmet from Garner and his chewing became even more frantic. He must have been in for about half-hour, mostly bobbing and weaving and ducking—and chewing. Then, suddenly, he wasn't chewing any more as finally it dawned on him he hadn't put any chewing gum in his mouth on his way out!

He had a rather sheepish smile on his face as he looked back to the dressing room to signal for a pack—but he never got one. A couple of balls later, I caught him off Malcolm. He wasn't chewing as he walked off, but I'm sure he was smiling. It was a rough initiation into Test cricket for him and the dressing room was a much safer place than the middle of Sabina Park.

Fast bowlers, I've learned over the years, are usually aggressive characters once they set foot on the ground, feel that ball in their grasp and glare at the batsman at the other end. They can be mean and some have long memories—such as Sylvester Clarke, who played a few Tests for the West Indies before disqualifying himself by going off to South Africa. Since then, he's been tormenting batsmen in the English county championship where he plays for Surrey and in the South African tournament.

Having played against 'Silly' in our own Shell Shield and toured Australia with him in 1981-82, I knew he had that aggressive streak that was typical of most fast bowlers. Even so, I was a little taken aback when he greeted Paul Allot with a screaming bouncer first ball in a festival match at Sabina Park back in 1982. Allott, the Lancashire and England fast bowler, was batting at No.9 for an International XI against a West Indies XI in the main, four-day match of the annual Air Florida Jamaica Festival and everything had been conducted at a fairly leisurely pace up until then.

Curious, I went up to Clarke at the end of the over and asked what was the reason for the sudden change of attitude.

"Well, he let me have a bouncer in the first county match last season when we played against Lancashire and I owed him one!" he explained.

by
Colin
Milburn

A TON OF CHEEK

MY cricketing career has been a mixture of a lot of highs and a few lows, but permanently imprinted on my mind is the day Sir Harry Secombe literally swept me off my feet.

There I was quietly enjoying a convivial lunch hosted by the Lord's Taverners, with Prince Philip doubling as Guest of Honour and 12th man. Harry, that incredible Goon and a past president of the Taverners, was also quietly enjoying himself at the prestigious affair. And he was about to become the star of the show.

The proposer of the main toast remarked it was the first time he had found himself seated between a 'couple of bookends', referring to Harry and me, and our bulk. Harry responded immediately in the most unexpected way.

He got out of his seat, strode up to mine, grabbed me and slung all 18½ stone (yes that's what I was in those days) over his shoulder. Then he carried me around the room in a fireman's lift, boldly declaring: "A couple of bookends, are we? Can anyone else do this?"

To this day I don't know how he managed it. Maybe the claret helped. When he finally put me down, I

detected an anxious glance from Prince Philip,
apparently fearful not even royalty was exempt from
Harry's buffoonery. Protocol prevailed. His Royal
Highness was allowed to remain seated.

NOBBLED DOWN UNDER

YOU could say it didn't take me long to discover what
a knock-out place Australia is after I arrived in 1966,
full of resolve to do my bit for Western Australia in
the Sheffield Shield.

In England I had suffered the ignominy of being
dropped from the Test team against the West Indies.
The invitation from Western Australia was just the
pick-me-up I needed.

So I arrived in Perth, taking my first-ever steps on
Aussie soil, determined to lose weight and promising
to cut back on the booze. I was met at the airport
by Western Australian cricket officials. It was a Tuesday
night and I thought, "Great, I'm not expected at the
first practice session until Saturday. Just think of it,
three days of sightseeing can't be bad."

We drove to the hotel, past magnificent skyscraper
buildings and into more humble surrounds. Never mind,
I thought, not too many distractions - ideal for a man
ready to renounce all vices and get back into shape.

The hotel was run by a typical down-to-earth Aussie,
Bill Watson.

The next morning I was up early and couldn't believe
my eyes when I went into the bar. It was full of hard-

working blokes from the bush—the sort who graft for nine months and enjoy themselves for the next three.

But hell, I thought, they were all drinking bloody milk. What sort of 'nancy boy' place had I come to? Was the image of the beer-swilling Aussie a myth manufactured in England? I quickly discovered this milk was whisky and milk. It was an aperitif! Well, if you can't beat 'em, join 'em. And I did.

Through to lunch time when the beer came out, and on to closing, 10pm.

The next morning I woke with a gigantic headache and feeling as sick as a dog. I was a write-off for the next two days. The only thing I saw in 48 hours was the inside of my hotel room. It was a good reminder I told myself, to steer clear of Australian milk or, at least avoid bad ice cubes.

On the Saturday I ambled gingerly to the opening practice session of the season. The secretary Les Truman, came up to me and asked if I had enjoyed my refreshing sightseeing break.

"Well, yes and no." I certainly hadn't seen anything of Perth, having been flat on my back. "Think I somehow managed to pick up a virus." Sympathy all round, and, the practice went well: I hit just about everything off the middle of the bat!

It was during my West Australian sojourn that I first clapped eyes on that phenomenal Aussie cricketing star, Greg Chappell. It still makes me smile. Greg was a 17-year-old kid trying to make his way for South Australia. We at Western Australia had four of their wickets down for next to nothing and Chappell was at the crease.

No problem. This pugnacious kid edged a ball to slip and that was the end of him—or so we thought. We just looked at the umpire who said 'not out' to our appeal. To our disbelief Greg did a Bill Lawry and didn't walk! I mean, here I was, an Englishman in Australia and everyone walked, didn't they? To us, he was clearly out, but a stick of dynamite wouldn't have shifted him.

We were now doubly determined to get the little bugger out. Tony Lock came on to bowl and I moved to forward short-leg. You should have heard the language from the pair of us. Not too gentlemanly! These were the wonderful days before that nasty sledging.

We were trying to un-nerve him with all the names under the sun. It was enough to make an old soldier blush, never mind an inexperienced kid. Greg never flinched—it was like water off a duck's back and he just got on with it.

You knew then he had the temperament for the big time.

On that tour I also quickly discovered some tricks the Aussies seem to have perfected. In Western Australia's last match of the season against New South Wales at Perth, they had a great chance of landing the Sheffield Shield by beating us. But, with one day to go, they only had one wicket standing and an overall lead of around 250. That meant we had to be favourites to cut short their celebrations.

Well, the night before the final day's play they threw a party. What splendid chaps I thought. Even more so when I discovered that I was the only player from the W.A. side they had chosen to invite. As a solid professional, I decided to limit myself to one drink all night but still enjoy the evening.

I swear to this day I only had one glass—the problem apparently was that when I was talking to someone on my left, someone else on my right filled the glass every time I was in danger of seeing the bottom of it. Little did I know that N.S.W. felt I was the danger man to their title hopes and they had, in great Aussie tradition, set out to nobble me.

The next morning I arrived at the ground and thought, "Hell that one drink was mighty powerful!" But they must have wondered what they had done when I took a blinding catch at first slip to dismiss their last man!

I went into bat and before long they gave me a bouncer. It was on me just that little bit quicker than I anticipated, thick top edge—caught!

They went on to win. So remember, if you are the only member of a team invited to a party, think twice or three times about accepting if it is the opposition throwing the party; and give it even more thought if they happen to be Australians!

by Doug Walters

A Slow Boat to China

IF cricket one day 'takes off' in mainland China and becomes more popular there than rice, you can thank a bloke named Phil O'Sullivan.

Phil is President of the Waverly District Cricket Club in Sydney and had long nurtured a vision of converting the Chinese to our game.

He still sees that country as a potential cricketing superpower and I sincerely hope his dream comes true. But gee, did he have some trouble getting his campaign off the ground.

When I retired from first-class cricket in 1981, Phil phoned me, along with Tony Greig and other past and present Test and Sheffield Shield players and members of his club; and outlined his grand plan. It sounded like a good idea at the time and since he was offering my wife Caroline and me a free trip, I jumped at the invitation.

Phil had chosen his team, but he did mention a few loose ends he still had to tie up. As it turned out, the loose ends were the matters of finding a sponsor or two and getting visas and other necessary documentation. If you think the first was a problem, the second was almost insurmountable, since China allowed very few tourists in those days.

Phil was not easily daunted by either problem and began negotiations immediately. Alas, sponsors were not forthcoming.

I suppose that it wasn't really surprising when you think he was taking virtually a team of has-beens to introduce cricket to China. They were not exactly going to get great value for their money.

The All-China Sports Federation issued an invitation for the tour during Australia's off season in 1984.

We dutifully marked the dates in our diary and made sure the two weeks were kept free for our trip. I was always doubtful about the tour ever taking place, but everyone else seemed enthusiastic. About six weeks before our scheduled departure, the tour was cancelled for want of a sponsor. Not to worry, said the ever-optimistic Phil. We'd go next year.

The second year came and went with the same result. So did the third and fourth. But Phil kept trying and each year two weeks were reserved in our diary. We almost made it one year. The visas were all sorted out, but the sponsorship fell through again at the last minute. Another let down, but at least he had gone close this time and I duly reserved the dates again for the following year. No result, I'm afraid.

"That's it," I told Caroline. "Don't bother to reserve those dates for Phil next year." But sure enough, Phil was on the phone again, assuring her the tour would go ahead. And it actually did! I still wasn't confident until we were actually on the plane and taxing out onto the tarmac ready for take off, but Phil had achieved the final stage of his ambition. To his credit, all but one of the original tourists selected were with us.

Caroline and I had decided to take our second son, Lynton, with us. We thought it would broaden his education and lessen the burden on Caroline's mother, Lil, who was minding the other three at home. It was ironic that had the original tour gone ahead we were going to take our eldest son and leave "baby" Lynton with Lil. Fourex, Channel 7 Network and Adidas were the major sponsors and there were some other contributors from Phil's area. So we were fitted out in jackets and T-shirts to leave Australia looking like a representative team—even if we did only *look* the part.

Hong Kong was our first stop. All being well, it would be a very pleasant stop, with a warm-up game against Kowloon Cricket Club. I had a reputation to live up to so I had a drink on the flight. However, I didn't know what the record was between Sydney and Hong Kong so I didn't overdo it. Besides, my pace-maker, Rod Marsh, wasn't there. My fellow tourists obviously decided that I'd lost a bit of form since my retirement and that I should lift my game since the boys from Fourex were looking after us.

A harbour cruise had been arranged on the Bond Junk and we were invited to dinner on the Island of Lama. The trip was great, so relaxing sitting up the front of the junk in the warm night air watching the lights of Hong Kong. And dinner, Chinese-style seafood, couldn't be faulted. I had lifted my game totally on this particular evening, determined not to miss a minute of the superb hospitality which had been showered on us since the start of the tour.

At some stage during the trip I realised that I hadn't seen Lynton for a while. The harbour was getting a little rough—or it seemed that way to me—and I feared he might have been up the front of the junk with a few of the more courageous cricketers. I decided to check on his safety.

I wasn't so concerned that I put down my glass of wine or extinguished my cigarette; I just thought I'd wander casually up the stairs to the front deck. If you've ever been on a junk, you'll know that the railing doesn't go all the way around, and I had to pick the worst possible time to go for a walk. Just as I reached an unrailed section, we hit a big wave. Both hands were occupied, and there was no rail to grasp anyway, so I disappeared quite ungracefully over the side into the middle of Victoria harbour.

Irrespective of stories you may have heard, or the rumours Max Walker spreads about my swimming ability, I can actually make it from one side of a pool to the other, but the distance of those shore lights, and the wash of the boat which was dragging me under, gave me some doubts about my immediate future and the rest of the tour. But luck was with Doug Walters that night. A very alert captain had seen my cigarette disappear as I hit the water and ordered the junk "full astern" or something like that and had a lifebuoy over the side to me so fast that I never did get a chance to check out what was at the bottom of the harbour.

Caroline was not at all amused when I told her that it was salty. For a few frightening minutes she'd had visions of returning to Sydney a widow. A change of clothes and a few more cans of Fourex at a promotion we had to attend back on shore at midnight and I was primed to take on the Chinese at cricket. Mind you, Caroline kept a very close eye on me for the rest of the tour.

I didn't fare that much better with the bat in China than I had done in England, but it gave me an appetite for any future tours Phil O'Sullivan may decide to organise and manage.

And if the game ever does take on in China, how would you like to be a national selector? I mean, how do you select 12 from a couple of hundred million hopefuls?

ABOUT THE AUTHORS

ALLAN BORDER: captain of Australia, captain of Queensland, but best known as one of the world's premier batsmen until last summer when his part-time spinners demolished the West Indians.

FRANK TYSON: England fast bowler who stormed onto the world cricket scene with such ferocity in the 50s he was nicknamed 'Typhoon'.

GREG CHAPPELL: giant of a batsman who strode the world cricket stage for over a decade in which he never ceased to delight with his exquisite strokeplay. Did, however, have an underarm problem.

HENRY BLOFELD: best known in England as a cricket commentator, on radio and in the Press. But became so popular in Australia fans on the notorious S.C.G. Hill erected the Henry Blowfly Stand.

BILL LAWRY: Former Australian Captain and dour but gifted opening bat of the 60s who appears to have undergone a charisma transplant on the Nine Network where his commentary has become legendary for its enthusiasm.

DAVID GOWER: captain of England and Leicester. A graceful left-hand batsman who has a way with words as delightful as the range of shots he plays in the middle.

GEOFF LAWSON: nicknamed by his mates, 'Henry', after the legendary Australian story-teller. This Lawson's main claim to fame is still his fast bowling but he's showing promise in the other area.

ALLAN LAMB: bristling moustache, built like a boulder, hits like a hurricane . . . and likes scoring laughs at his team-mates' expense as much as he likes scoring runs.

MARTIN CROWE: a great batsman whose rise has coincided with that of New Zealand in the world cricket rankings. Thinks he can play tennis, too.

ROD MARSH: early in his career he was called 'Iron Gloves'; at the end it was 'Golden Gloves', indeed a suitable accolade for the man who snared more victims than any other keeper.

VIV RICHARDS: he's called The Master Blaster but he's built like Mr. Universe. He and his team are in such good form they are The Masters of cricket's universe.

IAN WOOLDRIDGE: rated by many as the world's premier sports' columnist, but has a particular affinity to cricket, especially the Ashes battles.

RICHARD HADLEE: once got so ill in India he refused to go back; when he finally did this incredible Kiwi took enough wickets to become the world's highest wicket-taker. One of the best-ever bowlers.

BARRY RICHARDS: blond, and one of the most beautiful batsmen many in the world never got to see because of his South African nationality. He always had so much time to play his shots, the mark of the true genius.

SIR GARFIELD SOBERS: in an English County game he once hit all six balls in an over for six! But this great West Indian batsman, bowler and fieldsman had earned the accolade of World's Greatest Allrounder long before that indulgence.

PETER ROEBUCK: opens the batting for Somerset in English County cricket, but best known in Australia for his musings on the game in many of Australia's National Newspapers.

DAVID HOOKES: bombastic left-hand batsman whose brazen bludgeoning of Tony Greig's bowling in the Centenary Test, 1977, earned for him a reputation he may have preferred to do without. Outspoken on the game's future direction.

IAN BOTHAM: blessed with big, big biceps that contribute mightily to his hearty allround deeds ... and an even bigger heart which has ensured his charity walks contribute thousands of dollars to leukaemia research.

DAVID BOON: tough-as-teak Tasmanian who is now one of Australia's most consistent batsmen. His partnership with fellow opener Geoff Marsh is now as well known as was Simpson and Lawry.

RICHIE BENAUD: great Australian captain and allrounder, commentator for the BBC and the Nine Network, and a contributing columnist to major newspapers around the world.

DESMOND HAYNES: fans love this easy-going, likeable West Indian opening batsman whose style, first displayed against Australia at Antigua in 1978, earned him the appropriate nickname 'Hammer'.

BOB WILLIS: one of England's most successful opening bowlers. Crowds warmed to Willis for his courage in the face of physical adversity, for his unusual action and his Beatle-like hairstyle.

IAN CHAPPELL: 'Chappelli' was cricket's tough guy of the 70s, at the crease with a bat in his hand, or tactically after the toss of the coin. Now a Nine Network commentator where his views are as uncompromising.

SUNIL GAVASKAR: once was the captain of India, still is the biggest rungetter in Test cricket with over 10,000. Only small in stature, but big on ability and endless concentration.

IMRAN KHAN: the Pakistan captain which not only calls for cricket nous, but political instinct as well. Terribly good looking, according to polls among women, terribly good at cricket according to his cricketing peers.

DENNIS LILLEE: One of the greatest fast bowlers of all time! He had it all, pace, variation, aggression, instinct. Famous also for an impromtu sales convention for aluminium bats during a Test match against England.

ALAN KNOTT: chirpy little England wicket-keeper who endeared himself to cricket fans by indulging in seemingly impossible stretching exercises during games.

MERV HUGHES: the owner of cricket's most famous moustache, circa 1989, and a strange convict-like haircut circa 1789, to boot. Also bowls fast enough to have a bold cricketing future.

CLIVE LLOYD: once opened the bowling for the West Indies in the days when Spin was King. Since devoted his energies to brilliant batting and fielding, astute captaincy, and, finding and nurturing lots of fast bowlers.

JEFF THOMSON: one of the fastest, most dangerous and terrifying bowlers the world has seen. No batsman could adjust to the unpredictability, nor the sharp lift, of his delivery by way of a strange windmilling action.

GORDON GREENIDGE: when cricketing grandfathers tell grandsons about the great opening partnerships of the world they'll always mention Greenidge and Haynes first. Greenidge is an imposing sight as he favours the cut and hook against the pacemen.

LANCE CAIRNS: built a bit like the strongest man in the logging camp, this Kiwi could make the ball talk when he bowled, and make it fairly whistle when he hit it with his special heavyweight bats.

ASHLEY MALLETT: he was the offspinner during Australian cricket's Successful Seventies, usually getting the ball when Thomson, Lillee, Walker, Pascoe or Gilmour got tired. So, like all spinners, has a sense of humour.

DEREK UNDERWOOD: nicknamed 'Deadly' with good reason. His devious, swiftish left-arm spin fatally wounded many a good batting side caught with its feet stuck in an English mud pie pitch.

JOHN MORRISON: when he came into bowl against Australia in a one-day international and did well Dennis Lillee dubbed him 'Mystery Morrison'. Better remembered as a solid opening and middle-order batsman for New Zealand.

JEFF DUJON: West Indian wicket-keeper during the decade in which fast bowling became an art form. Not only is he noted for his acrobatic glovework, he is a fine batsman.

COLIN MILBURN: rather jovial, portly England opening batsman who believed in taking the attack to the bowler, and therefore a crowd-pleaser. Career ended by a tragic car smash.

DOUG WALTERS: The Boy From Dungog. Before he wrote the sporting best-seller, *One For The Road*, his main claim to fame was as a magnificent batsman in the 70s. Oh, and a plea of guilty to liking a smoke and a drink!